John Buchan was born in 1875 in Pei
Childhood holidays were spent in the B
great love. His passion for the Scottish countryside is reflected in
his writing. He was educated at Glasgow University and Brasenose
College, Oxford, where he was President of the Union.

Called to the Bar in 1901, he became Lord Milner's assistant
private secretary in South Africa. In 1907 he was a publisher with
Nelson's. In World War I he was a *Times* correspondent at the
Front, an officer in the Intelligence Corps and adviser to the War
Cabinet. He was elected Conservative MP in one of the Scottish
Universities' seats in 1927 and was created Baron Tweedsmuir in
1935. From 1935 until his death in 1940 he was Governor
General of Canada.

Buchan is most famous for his adventure stories. High in
romance, these are peopled by a large cast of characters, of which
Richard Hannay is his best known. Hannay appears in *The Thirty-
nine Steps*. Alfred Hitchcock adapted it for the screen. A TV series
featured actor Robert Powell as Richard Hannay.

JOHN BUCHAN
SIR WALTER RALEIGH

HOUSE OF
STRATUS

This edition published in 2008 by House of Stratus, an imprint of
Stratus Books Ltd., 21 Beeching Park, Kelly Bray,
Cornwall, PL17 8QS, UK.

www.houseofstratus.com

Typeset, printed and bound by House of Stratus.

A catalogue record for this book is available from the British Library.

ISBN 07551-171-8-2

CONTENTS

To Master George Edward Brown

My Dear Ted,

You have given me the permission to put your name in this book, so I owe it to you to explain its purpose. It is a life of Sir Walter Raleigh, told in eleven stories. I have taken the chief scenes in his life, and made some friend or follower write about them as if he had seen them with his own eyes. I do not know of there was ever a Gervase Luttrell or a Nathan Stubbs, but I know that people just like them lived in Raleigh's day, and saw and heard the things they write about here. So, though I have invented some of the characters, all that they tell us really happened, and most of the little incidents and speeches will be found recorded in the old books. It is a story, but an "owner true" story, and you must not think that it only came out of my head.

It is intended for all sorts of people to read, but especially for boys. Sir Walter Raleigh is the most boyish hero in history. Till his head fell on the block he never lost his eager, generous interest in life. He was planning great adventures when other men are dull and middle-aged. His heart was always young – and that is a very different thing from being childish. He made many mistakes, and paid heavily for them; but no misfortunes could crush his spirit. When all that he had built fell about his ears, he set patiently to work to build it up anew. Like a great modern poet, he

"Held we fall to rise, are baffled to fight better,
   Sleep to wake."

He had almost every talent. He was a brilliant courtier, a gallant soldier and sailor, a great discoverer, a very wise statesman, a learned scholar, and a true poet. No man ever got more out of life, both joy and sorrow. He was never afraid to take risks, for he thought that achievement was cheaply purchased by suffering. His story, if we look at it in one way, is a tragedy, for all his ventures seemed to fail, and after weary years in prison he died on the scaffold. But, properly considered, it is a happy tale, for he never lost heart, and disaster never conquered his courage. He sowed the seed which bore fruit long after his time. It was the example and the teaching of Raleigh that first set our people forming colonies in new lands. The British Empire of today, and the Republic of the United States, are alike built on his dreams. So you see that after all he fulfilled the purpose of his life, and gave to the English race "better Indies than the King of Spain's."

Your affectionate friend,

JB

CHAPTER 1

The Luterano [1]
(1564)

"Still climbing trees in the Hesperides."
Love's Labour's Lost, iv. 3.

'Twas in the summer of 1564, I think, that I first got a hint of the quality of my playfellow. Our land in those days was at peace with Spain; but both sides watched each other like sheep dogs at a fair, waiting to spring on the first show of offence. For had not that gracious and magnificent lady, our Queen Gloriana, scoffed at the suit of His Catholic and Spanish Majesty, who was little used to rebuffs from man or woman? Likewise, the Queen of Scots was threatening alarums from the north, so it became all good lovers of England to keep their blades keen against evils to come. We were a band of five in the Otter valley, lads much of an age: myself, the eldest, not yet turned of thirteen. There was Dick Champernoun from Clyst, the hardest hitter and the lustiest of the bank. I see yet his yellow tumbled hair, and the steady grey eyes which death glazed five years later on the field of Montcontour. There was Humphrey Sneyd from ten miles up the water, who would ride down on a pony to our Saturday's sports with tales of the moormen and the outlandish ways of the hill country. There was

1

Harry Duke, too, from Otterton, a silent lad, and the best to handle a boat I have ever known. Indeed, his true fellows were the sailor folk of Budleigh; for any hours he could snatch from his schooling he was off to the bass-fishing, or driving his little ketch in the worst gales of our parts. He had been east to Poole and west to Plymouth, but already he was sated with our coasts and burned for the high seas.

And last there was Walter Raleigh from Hayes Barton, the youngest of the four, and as silent as Harry Duke, but with a different manner of silence. He was the only scholar in our band, and turned to his books as readily as to a horse or a full river. He had a fine virginal face, with the soft colour of a maid, and a low delicate voice. But there was that in his blue eyes which kindled at times into naked devilry; and at such seasons, though the youngest, none dared gainsay his leadership. 'Twas he who first leaped the awful chasm called Tamsin's Gap, and one winter day swam the roaring Otter because I had questioned his valour. 'Twas he, too, who at Bixton Fair, when the sailors and the moormen came to blows, headed a rally with a blunt hanger and sent the hill-folk scurrying out of the town.

But to my tale. The summer of the year I speak of was hot and dry, so that we lads from the landward parts were fain to go often to the shore to swim and get the cool airs from the water, while we watched for great ships passing out Channel. Now at the little port of Budleigh there is an inn, The Flying Hinde its name, much frequented of merchants and travellers, and a place of resort, too, for the townsfolk and the neighbouring gentlemen. Opposite the inn, fronting on the sea, is a hillock of green grass with a little flagstaff atop of it, from which the eye has a noble prospect over the bay of Otter and into the narrow seas. It was a pleasant place of a summer afternoon, with the bees droning in the hot thyme and the gulls crying. The potman from The Flying Hinde would fetch tankards of ale, and any day about four o'clock you would find a bench of old seafarers telling tales of the great deep. To such tales we lads loved to listen – Dick and Humphrey each prone on his face with a stem of grass between his lips, Harry walking restlessly with his eyes on the sea, and Walter Raleigh sitting with hands clasping knees, his gaze dwelling hungrily on the face of the narrator.

On this afternoon there were but two on the hill. One was Noah Stubbs, an ancient sailorman, wanting the left arm, whose family dwelt in Budleigh. Noah was something of an oracle to us younger folk, for he had adventured far in his travels, had seen the Main, and dealt lusty blows in the Spanish isles. A round shot in the Azores had carried off an arm, and, being turned sixty and well-to-do from his ventures, he had settled in a cottage with a venerable mother to spend his last years in peace. He was a square-set, brawny fellow, very deep in the chest, with a swarthy countenance and great black eyes like a Spaniard. He had hoops of gold in his ears, and bracelets of copper and golden wire at his wrist. His dress in summer-time was no more than a shirt and old breeches of seaman's cloth, below which his great knotted legs stood out like oak-trees. He had a habit of chewing some herb, so that his teeth were yellow as doubloons.

The other was a stranger who came twice or thrice a year to our port, and dealt with the country folk in foreign merchandise. He was a Frenchman out of Brittany, a man on Noah's years but more fallen in his age. Master Laurens they called him, and all Budleigh paid him respect, for he had an eye that commanded it. He captained a merchant barque, but no man knew his home or his history, save that he was of the Reformed religion, and had fallen out with the French king in the matter of his faith. There were some said he had been a rover in the western seas and had repented of his sins; others, that he had escaped from the Spanish galleys; while others would have it that he was a noble of France who for state reasons came to us as a plain sea-captain. There was that in his grave, manly carriage that spelled gentility, if I am any judge of it. He spoke our tongue well, and would often sit within or without The Flying Hinde, listening to Noah's tales of his deeds, but himself speaking little.

This day Noah was full of memories. He had sailed with Master William Hawkins, father of the great Sir John, in his ship *Pola*, of Plymouth, to the African coast in quest of negroes, and had been ashore on nigh every isle of the Indies. He deplored the might of the Spaniard, and condemned his insolence.

"Look ye," he cried, "he claims the whole West in the name of Christ, and yet his deeds smell rankly to Heaven. What English blood can stomach the taunt? If we so much as put our nose inside his Isles, the odds are we are shown the door with half of our hulls blown off. Is it fit that the golden wealth of the Indies should go to fatten the Pope and his priests? The reckoning comes, I tell you," and he spat fiercely on the ground.

Walter Raleigh up and asked him about this wealth, and Noah's tongue grew looser.

"Ha'n't I seen it with my own eyes? I ha' been in Porto Bello at the summer Fair, when all the treasure of the Indies is brought together. I ha' seen the streets piled with silver ingots like causeway stones, and mule teams from Panama bringing every hour quintals of gold. Look ye, young masters, there be no end to the riches of those lands. Merchants walk the place like kings, and the Spanish Governors are more magnifical than any Emperor. Down from the mountains of New Granada comes emeralds as big as roundshot. There are pearls from Margarita, and cacao and costly herbs from Cartagena, and dyewoods from New Spain. Ay, and gold from the length and breadth of the Main, as plenteous as herrings on Budleigh Quay. There be a great king's ship, you must know, called the *Navio del Oro*, which plies from Panama to Callao, and collects King's tribute on that coast. They fetch it over the isthmus on mules, and oft I ha' longed for a hundred Devon men to wait snugly at a corner of the road. And out in the roadstead you may see the fleets of Spain, twenty war vessels with fifty guns apiece, awaiting to bear the treasure home. I ha' seen the General of the Galleons – they call him General, which be a strange name for a sailorman – come ashore in a pinnace with rowers in steel and scarlet, and a cloth o' gold on the thwart, and negresses a-waving palm-leaves to cool the air. Maybe you ha' seen the sight, Master Laurens?"

The Frenchman shook his head. "I have never been to Porto Bello. But I have seen the Almirante of the Flota come ashore at San Juan d'Ulloa in somewhat less state. He swam, with his arm on a spar, what time his flagship foundered."

Noah laughed. "The hand of God was not idle that day, camarado. Would that it moved oftener, for the sinking of a fleet or two would ease His Catholic Majesty of a little pride."

Some of us lads asked why, if such rich argosies sailed the seas, there were no enemies of Spain at hand to trouble them. I think we all dreamed that capturing a Spaniard was as easy as spearing a flounder in the Otter mouth.

"They keep together," said Noah, "like the moormen at Bixton Fair. Nothing less than a dozen great ships of war could master the Galleons, and till Queen Bess fights King Philip the sight will not be seen. But we corsarios have adventured against single vessels, and oftentimes cut off a lesser ship. I mind at the Isle o' Pines – But indeed I fear to speak of violent doings in your presence, master."

The Frenchman smiled pleasantly. " 'Twas an honest cause and a clean war," he said. "The hearing will do these lads no ill, and I am too old and worn to be corrupted."

"Well, 'twas but a little thing," said Noah, nothing loth. "We had no better craft than a frail patache – myself, Tom Carey of Bideford, an Irishman called Bourke, the Frenchman Jean Terrier, and four Indians from the Logwood coast. Our haven was the River of St John in Florida, but we laid up like other venturers at the Isle o' Pines, under the lee of Cuba, and waited for what fortune God might send us. We watched the tall Galleons staggering up with the land wind to round old St Antonio, and danced for grief that we must let 'em pass unhindered. There they were, like a flock of swans, crammed to the bilge with gold, while we hungry Christians sat on a hot rock and cursed 'em. We durstn't venture, for one shot amidships would have sunk our crazy patache. We had captured her but a month before in the Bahamas, and she was foul and rotten with ill handling. For us to outface a navy was madder than for a sprat to charge a shoal of whales. So we waited and banned 'em.

"The Galleons went down seas and out of sight, and presently comes another craft in their wake. In a trice I see what she was. She was the General's azogue, which had gone to Campeachy for the Tabasco tribute, and was now in a hurry to get up with her convoy. The silly thing had blundered too far south on her long tack. Then she had catched sight of the Galleons to the east, and swung round and come down wind after 'em.

"We knowed it was the chance of our lives, and were in a stew to get started. We run the patache out into the wind with oars, and swooped down on the azogue like a fish-hawk. For a moment we thought she had the heels of us, and so she had if the lubbers aboard her had been seamen. Moreover, had she stopped to fight, she might ha' blown us out of the water, for we carried but two old guns, which would have missed a mountain at a catapult's length. But she were mad with fear, and held her course without a shot till we scraped her side and skipped over her bulwarks. Two hundred quintals of silver, camarados – two hundred thousand honest English pounds, besides a good store of ducats. We towed her back to our island, where we marooned the Spaniards, and in three days got some kind of crew in her and sailed her back to English seas. Fourteen blessed weeks the voyage lasted, and Jean Terrier's leg had come off along of a spar crushing it, whence ever after the Spaniards called him 'Pie de Palo.' That's all my tale masters. Now that I ha' run into port for good, 'tis a kind of comfort to reflect that I once had a Governor of Campeachy plucking seafowls for my dinner."

One of us asked him if he had ever fought the Spaniard at greater odds, for ship against ship seemed to us dull fighting.

"Not I," said Noah. "They are better armed and manned than us, and 'twould have been tempting Providence too far to risk further odds. We were weak with eating rotten flesh and drinking foul water, and sweating 'neath a sun whose every beam is charged with fever. Would you have us add to Heaven's hardships? Besides, we loved not to fall into the Spaniard's hands, for his tender mercies were cruel. At the best 'twas the galleys of Cadiz or glorifying God on the faggots in Valladolid Square. At the worst 'twas such torments as only fiends dream of." Noah, smiling grimly, bared his single arm and showed a long straggling seam from the wrist nigh almost to the shoulder. "The tale of that beauty mark won't bear telling to young ears," he said.

I noted that Walter Raleigh's face had kindled. "Was there no man among you," he asked, "bold enough to captain the corsarios and make a fleet of your little ships?"

"I ha' heard of but one," Noah answered, "and he left the seas long time ago. I never clapped eyes on him, but his name was as famous as King Philip's. Nay, not his name, for I never heard it, but a byname the Spaniards gave him. They called him 'The Luterano,' for he was a Frenchman of the Reformed faith and mightily incensed against the Pope. But withal he was a just man and a merciful, selling back his captives like a Christian for good gold, and never wantonly affronting a poor man. In truth, even in the Spanish lands, the common people praised him, for he would plunder the Almirantes and give a good tithe in charity to those they had grinded down. I ha' seen his topsails in the Bahama Keys, and 'twas a comfortable sight to watch the caravels and barques running for shelter to the forts like pullets when a sparrow-hawk hovers. I once shipped alongside his first seaman, a man out of Cornwall, an honest lad but full of fierce oaths. He had tales – yea, by Harry's soul, he had tales."

Noah stopped and hunted in the pouch of his breeches for some of the herb he chewed. He pretended to be afraid of Humphrey, who would have beaten him for his slow speech. "Mercy, brave sir, you melt my old bones. You look like the Luterano himself, when I saw him singe the beards of the Dons in Habana tideway."

"But I thought you said you had never seen him," I put in.

"In a manner of speaking I ha' not, and again in a manner of speaking I have. Leastways I ha' seen his ship, and I ha' seen him fight. 'Twas in Habana, where for my sins I was carrying cut stone on the harbour wall along of blackamoors and Indians. An ill wind up in the Florida Keys had brought down on us a Spanish ship of war while we were all sick to death of the fever. She sank our craft, and with it my poor honest comrades, but I floated till a Spaniard grabbed my hair and haled me aboard. They took me to Habana, where I was fed on offal and set to toil with the Almirante's slaves. 'Twas a grim task to sweat there in the steaming noons with the whip flicking off patches of your hide should you halt even to wipe your forehead. I was sunk in melancholy, for I mourned for my dead comrades, and but for a confident hope in God' charity, would ha' leaped, shackles and all, into the sea.

"I ha' told you ere this of my escape through the merciful dispensation of an earthquake. But what I tell now happened in the blackest days of my captivity, and gave me grace to pluck up heart. One morning there came a rumour among us slaves of a bold deed at Chagre on the Main. It seemed that the Lord Viceroy of Panama had sent his own caravel to Hispaniola for horses, and that the loaded ship was on the point of making Chagre when up comes our friend the Luterano. His craft was ever a swift patache, in which he would strike down the greatest vessel that sailed the sea. In half an hour he had the Viceroy's crew under the hatches, and presently all the horses were in the water swimming to land. The Luterano wanted no plunder, but only a seaworthy craft to oblige a friend. He dropped the Spaniards into the caravel's cock-boats to make the shore at their leisure, and upped sails and made for the seas. Here was a pretty singeing of His Majesty's beard, and there was hue and cry along the Main, and ships of war watching all the gates of the Isles. But never a trace could they find of the Luterano. Word came that a merchant had seen his sails off Margarita, and next morn there would be news of him from Campeachy. He spirited about these seas as if he were verily that Father of Lies the Dons believed him. We poor souls on the harbour wall heard the rumour of the tale and laughed at the jest of it, little witting that we were to see with our own eyes the next move of our brave gentleman.

"A week later, one blistering midday, there rose a great crying from some small craft in the harbour. You must know, sirs, that the bay of Habana is a narrow one at the mouth, and runs far inland, growing shallower as it nears its head. The fort and city lie on one side of this bay, and on the other is a green swampy shore with much forest. We could see a light patache anchored there, and every merchant captain in the port shaking his fist at her and shouting that 'twas the Luterano. And sure enough she flew at her masthead the French lilies.

" 'Twas like a mad dog, that every one shouts on his neighbour to kill but none durst go near. The patache lay peacefully at anchor, and a man on her deck played a little air on a tabor. There were five Spanish ships of war in the bay, but so great was the terror of the stranger that not one of the five – or all of them together – ventured near her. So there he might have lain as long as he pleased had it not been for the citizens of Habana, and especially my task-master, the Almirante of the port, who was determined the corsario should not escape him. So he summons the captains of the Spanish ships, and bids them at any cost take the Luterano, and promises to pay for any hurt done in the attempt to ships or men. Two captains refused, but three were so shamed by the Almirante that they assented to do his bidding, and sailed down on the little patache.

"The wind blew off the farther shore, and long ere the warships could tack across, the Luterano was fleeing for the upper end of the bay. He knew to an inch the depth of water, and scudded over shoals and bars where no heavier craft could follow. There he anchored, while a quarter mile outside the Spaniards halted and shot at him with their great guns. They never came near him, but continued the salvo till nightfall, and then, having a fear lest he should board them in the dark, they returned to Habana.

"Next day 'twas the same. The five warships – for the other two by now had plucked up courage – sailed up with the tide and fired guns all the day. The shots fanned in the air, maybe, into a pleasant coolness, but did not scrape a finger of paint from the little patache. A company of soldiers came round by land and would have rowed out to her, but her guns deterred 'em. The game was pleasant for the Luterano, for he had good anchorage, sweet water nigh at hand on the shore, and the spectacle of his foes and their foolishness.

"The morning after, a hurricane blew down on us from the nor'-east, and the shipping in the port was like to break its moorings. The warships did not venture out, for their crews were as lubberly sailors as they were vile marksmen. They lay tied up to the shore with cables, one hull pounding on the other, while we on the harbour wall toiled in the teeth of the gale, thanking Heaven for the cool weather. Presently out of the scud we could see a little patache with every sail set and a bank of men at the sweeps, striving to get clear up the bay. 'Twas friend Luterano, weary of sitting on a mud bank. He had no time or room to tack, but trusted to the broad backs of his crew.

"Instantly there was a commotion among the warships. And the three that had attacked the first day made haste to pursue. They cut their cables at the slack and plunged down wind after the patache. Now you must know that the tide in a nor'-easter in the port runs monstrous hard; and what with the wind on the beam, and the furious waves and bad handling, all three were like to have foundered. By this time the patache was in the throat of the bay, and the ships of war, thinking her capture beyond hope, and being fearful of their lives, endeavoured to return. But they could not bring the vessels round, and the crews, falling into a panic, lowered the boats and made for the shore. One boat was swamped, but the other cargoes of tallow-chandlers came safe to port.

"Presently the Luterano, casting a look back, saw how things were shaping. He observed three deserted ships of war tossing in the tideway, and being a thrifty man sought to salve them. By

Harry's soul, 'twas a sight to see how he drove his little ship in the teeth of a full gale and swollen sea. We on the harbour wall cheered him lustily, for in the confusion of the wind none could hear us. He secured all three ships, while their crews watched him from the town. Having no need of a fleet, he laid a train of powder and set two of 'em alight. They blazed like a pharos as the wind caught their top-gear, and settled down on the lee shore to smoulder half the night. Meantime the Luterano put some of his men in the third and best of the ships, and sailed off to the Florida Straits to lie in wait for His Majesty's Galleons."

Harry Duke tossed his cap into the air. "Bravo!" he cried. "There was a man and a seaman! Would we had more of his breed!"

Master Laurens smiled and shook his head. " 'Tis a good tale, Noah, but in one matter you err. I, too, have heard of your Luterano, and he cared little for the Galleons of Spain. He sought, like many adventurers, a bigger prize."

Walter Raleigh, whose eyes never left the Frenchman's face, asked him what that was.

"A new world," he said softly. "He cared little to harry Spain, though 'twas a righteous work enough. But he burned all his days – nay, burneth still if he is above the ground – for a new Indies, where the Spaniard hath never trod. The West is full of the tales of it."

"Ay, ay," Noah broke in; "I too have had my hunt for El Dorado. I got a chart once out of Master Potter of Bristol, the true tale of one Tom Medlicot, with the bearings and soundings shown. But by following it I ran into the claws of Almirante of New Spain, and lost chart and ship, and all but the breeches I stood in. I ha' never touched at El Dorado, masters, but I ha' seen such a place afar off when wind and tide suffered me to come no nearer."

We asked him the whereabouts of the country. "Tis a week's journey nor'-nor'-by-east of the River of St John. There is a multitude of islands, green as England, with air as sweet as Devon moor, and all manner of fine pastures and orchard land. There are no fevers such as scourge the Main, and no hurtful beasts, and the soil is so good that a man may harvest twice a year. I had thoughts of planting myself there to wear out my old age, but the winds drove me off, and ere I could try again King Philip had laid hold on me. I ha' heard also from an Indian at Campeachy of a land in the mountains in the West where the sand of rivers is gold, such as you read of in Holy Writ. But all Indians be mighty liars."

"You have been to El Dorado, Master?" Raleigh asked the Frenchman.

"I have seen it," said the old man, "or what I took to be it, but only afar off, like Moses from Pisgah."

We were clamorous to know more of this Promised Land, and Master Laurens, wetting his finger with ale, drew a plan of it on the little table by which he sat. 'Twas Hebrew to us lads, but we gathered that the place lay in the south part of the Americas which the Spaniards call Tierra Firme, and many hundred miles south of the Main. It seemed there was a great river which Master Laurens called the Orinoko, a river as wide as our Narrow Seas. At first it flowed among salt marshes, and then as you travelled up its stream you came to great forests where strange beasts dwelt and stranger men. And after weeks and maybe months of travel, when the river had grown little, you came to uplands full of flocks and herds and fields of grain, and great Indian towns where gold and silver were of no account for commonness. And last of all, when the river was no more than a stream, came the high mountains. Far up in a vale of them is a cataract. And beyond the fall a great valley set among cliffs. That is the true El Dorado, for in that valley is the greatest and richest city of earth. The folk in it are as white as we of England, and noble in stature and countenance. They worship the one God in a temple whose roof is solid beaten gold, and all the streets are of marble and red jasper.

Breathless, we asked him if he had had a glimpse of this marvel.

"After many weary wanderings," he said, "I and three comrades came to the top of a high mountain and we saw the valley afar off. We were faint with fever and hunger, and the sight revived our hearts. But there was no way to it from that mountain, for round the valley is a girdle of cliffs which only a bird may pass. For ten days we laboured to no avail, and then famine drove us back to the plain. One man of us would not return, but what befell him, whether he died or attained the city, I know not. Long after, I heard from an Indian of those parts that there is but one way to El Dorado. A man must ascend the river and find the track to climb the cataract. But the path is a secret kept by the people of the City, and though 'tis known to a few Indians of the plains none durst reveal it."

The tale set our fancies aflame, and Walter Raleigh in especial could sit still no longer.

"We will make a band among us to enter the Golden City," he cried, and we four assented, while Noah sat laughing, and the old Frenchman looked at us beneath his brows.

" 'Tis a road many have trod and none have mastered," he said.

"Ay," said Walter "but we will tread it with a single heart from our first manhood. Though we win to it with bent backs and silvered hair, yet win to it we shall."

The Frenchman smiled.

"And when you win to it, what will you do?" he asked.

"Then," said Walter, taking off his hat and bowing low, "I will give our gracious lady, the Queen of England, a better Indies than ever the King of Spain hath."

That was the first time I heard the saying which later was often on my comrade's lips, and indeed was the maxim of his life.

Master Lauren approved. He nodded gravely. "I think there is that in your brow, lad, and in your eyes which spells fortune. It may be good or ill, but 'twill be a high fortune. I think you will win to the Indies and make much ado there; and if you do not win to El Dorado, you will seek it all your days and leave the quest only at death."

Then he took from his pouch a little gold trinket such as a man may wear at his collar.

"You are of the breed I love, dear lad, and I will give you a charm to wear against ills to come. Mayhap 'twill bring you to your Promised Land, for 'tis from the tomb of a great King of the Indians who died long ago. It never brought me good luck, but it brought me joy in the quest, and I think that is the best fortune for a man. I cannot read the stars for you, but I can foretell one part of your fate. You will get great joy and sorrow out of life, but you will never lose the savour and zest of it."

There was that in the air and the occasion which held us silent. Walter Raleigh took the jewel, blushing boy-like a little, and stammering this thanks.

"Master, I will wear your gift all my days, but I would fain know the name of the giver."

The Frenchman smiled.

"If any man asks you that question in these parts, say the jewel came from Pierre Laurens of Le Havre, a merchant of silks and cloths, and owner of the barque *Saint Esprit*. But if any ask it you on the High Seas, or west of the Azores, or in the Isles, or on the Main, say that the giver was the Luterano."

1 This story was told by Sir John Buller, Knight, of Newkerne, in Devon to his grandson Jack, who when he grew older wrote it down in a book. A second Jack, great-grandson of the first, used to read it on summer Sunday afternoons to his nephews and great-nephews, one of whom remembered it and long afterwards told it to me.

CHAPTER 2

The Road of the Sunset [1]
(1581)

"We are those fools who could not rest
    In the dull earth we left behind,
But burned with passion for the West,
    And drank a frenzy from its wind;
The world where small men live at ease
    Fades from our unregretful eyes,
And blind across uncharted seas
    We stagger on our enterprise."

The Ship of Fools

…The country I travelled was as wild as nether limits of Muscovy. From the ill-marked track ran wastes of bog and stone, with shining pools of water scattered among them, and at intervals a roaring stream, brown as October ale. No human habitation appeared, though here and there was a charred patch of ground where may have stood one of the huts which my lord Grey had burned in his war with the Geraldines. Low hills, shaggy with dwarf trees, skirted the road at a distance of a mile or two, and held the morasses, as it were, in a cup. I had noted that for the last hour the little streams had taken the same direction as the track, so I looked presently to reach a river of some magnitude. Sure enough, as I came over a ridge I perceived a broad glen below me filled with a wood of oaks and hollies, and from somewhere in the thicket came the roar of swollen waters.

That morn I had set out from the town of Youghal to seek my Captain. A month before I had been appointed lieutenant to Captain Raleigh's foot-band, at the noble wage of two shillings a day. I had come hungry from the wars in the Low Countries, where under Sir John Norris I had for long been maintaining the cause of the Reformed religion and His Highness of Orange. The chance of Irish service offered me through the graces of my cousin at Court, my lady Dawtrey, was not to be scoffed at by a poor soldier. I had heard of the country as an excellent school of arms, where a man might win skill in his trade, albeit there was small hope of winning riches. Furthermore, I had a notion to serve under Captain Raleigh, the fame of whom was beginning to reach the ears even of us lean waiters upon Fortune. He was but a year or two my elder, and already had fought campaigns in France and Flanders; and had lately captained a ship with Humphrey Gilbert to fight the Spaniard. The news of his Irish doings had set the town ringing. For if Drury and Malby and my lord Grey had chastised the rebels with whips, this Raleigh had a taste for scorpions. The tale of the slaughter at Smerwick was so fierce that many of the stoutest – 'twas said even the Queen herself – thought the thing barbarously done. For myself, I love a fierce man who wars with his whole heart, and 'twas this whim of mine, as likewise my poverty, which had set me spurring this May morning to join my Captain.

I had scarce entered the shade of the oaks, when a man, running blindly down the steep, all but charged into my stirrups. He started back and would have fled, but I laid hold on his long hair and held it firm. He was a lath of a man, with famine burning in his eye-sockets, and in my hands was no stronger that a straw.

"Where away so hastily, my lad?" I said. But the creature shook his head; he knew not the English tongue. Then I gripped him by his ear.

"If this is treason," says I, "you will pay dear for it. Has Captain Raleigh passed this way?"

The name was familiar, for he nodded his head. "Rol-lee, Ro-lee," he repeated, and pointed down the road.

"Good," says I; "then here's a girdle-cake for your news." I tossed him food from my wallet, and left him squatted in the track, tearing it like a famished wolf.

Presently I saw ahead of me in the oak glade a little company of horsemen, and hailed them. They stopped as one man and wheeled, and the leader of them rode forward to greet me. This was the first time I had clapped eyes upon the great Walter Raleigh, destined ere long to be the most shining figure in Europe. He was a stalwart man, with a very proud carriage of the head, and a cheek browned by moorland wars. Save for his eyes, there was nothing to mark him out from other Captains of birth and mettle. But those eyes – I see yet the strange glint of them, as they looked into the heart of a man. I have never seen eyes so fearless and so keen. They were merry, too, as if, looking through one, he saw a pleasant landscape beyond. There was fire in them, the silent fire which glows in the white heart of the furnace and never sputters into flame. But above all there was pride, the pride which is so masterful that it asks for no recognition, which would condescend on kings and emperors, yea, on all things save Almighty God. In a flash I think I had the nature of the man, and his history has not proved me false. For this Captain was of so great a soul that he must look over the heads of other men and do his work stooping. Judge if a task be best done with a bowed back.

I think I hated him as his eyes ran me through. He asked me my name and warrant, nodding carelessly to my answer. Then he bade his men drop a bow-shot behind, while he and I rode ahead, and a frieze-clad kern trotted with us to show the way.

"A grim land," he said, looking round him. "Did you see aught of beast or man on your way from Youghal?"

I told him of the creature whose ear I had held at the edge of the oak-wood. He narrowed his eyes till they were like nuts seen through half-open shells – a way he always had when he reflected.

"I was warned of trouble," he said to himself. "Besides, the land was more than usual empty; 'twas like a graveyard. Do you think the fellow carried a message?" he asked.

"If he did, he could not carry it far," I answered. "He carried too little flesh on his bones. The thing was as frail as a new-born kitten."

I had heard of my Captain as very little compassionate. But now his face softened till, but for his beard, it might have been a handsome woman's.

"Ay, that is the curse on't. The innocent poor folk are starving. You will see them lie dead on the moss with half-chewed herbs in their teeth. And all the while the vermin of Rome grow fat, priests and Spaniards are in every hold, and the native lords are harsher oppressors than ever we English were. God knows I have never lifted my hand on one of the poor Irish, but God forget me if I spare and smite not the leeches that prey upon their blood."

By this time we were at the crest of a little hill in the forest, and saw below us the track running to a ford. 'Twas the river I had guessed the presence of, a swollen and angry current, with wood and thatch bobbing in its eddies. Around the ford was a close thicket of young hazels.

"We must swim, sir," I said; "and if you have any foes in the countryside, it is by that ford you must look for them."

"True, Mr Luttrell," he answered, a little smile playing round his mouth. " 'Tis a fine tryst for my ill-wishers. The scarecrow you met would be taking the tidings. There is a certain Fitz-Edmunds, whom they call in these parts the Seneschal of Imokelly. Haply he is down among the hazels. But I grieve to tell you that he is a cowardly knave, and would not come out to fight me with fewer than four hundred foot and horse. Now I do not think such a force could be levied within a hundred miles, so I fear we shall not meet the Seneschal."

"Were it not wise to wait for your troop, sir?" I ventured.

"Troop?" he cried. "Nay, lad, let's draw the coverts ourselves, and see if we can start an old fox."

His eyes suddenly grew light and wild as a boy's. He spurred his horse and galloped furiously down the track to the water, while I followed as best I could, leaving guide and troop to come on at their pleasure. We slithered among oak-roots and rasped through bramble thickets; my face was slashed by errant boughs, and many times I had like to have been on my nose. It seemed like a second's time from the brow of the hill till the first wash of the stream took my horse's pasterns.

That mad race was our salvation. There were watchers by the ford, but we were on them ere they looked for us. We were stemming the water before they could close in, and happily they had small store of arquebuses. Some half-dozen got before the Captain, and I saw his sword flash and the water redden. But I had little leisure to watch him, for, being second in the race, I received the larger part of the freebooter's notice. They clung to my saddle, and reached long arms for my bridle and the joints of my corselet. These were no kerns who assailed me, but foreign fellows with the dark cheek of Spain and Italy, the same as Alva had led to the pillage of the Hollanders. There was also one man, wearing a saffron jerkin over a cuirass, who sat his horse in the current and issued orders. I supposed him the Seneschal, and being very wroth I fired on him with my pistol. But the swaying and confusion gave me a poor aim, and the delay gave my assailants a chance, so that I had almost ended my Irish wars at the start of them.

I was torn from the saddle and dragged under the turbid stream, swallowing great draughts of water and mud. Choking and blinded, I found my feet at last and got my head above the current. But then I was in no better case. The river ran near my armpits, and that and the crush of men gave me no liberty to use my sword. 'Twas all a mad mellay of claw and tooth, a game which two dozen of the scum of Seville will play better than a lonely gentleman. Meantime I was aware of Captain Raleigh shaking himself on the farther bank, and bellowing for his troop to hasten. He seemed to have forgotten my case, so I minded him of it by a cry for succour. The next second he had taken the flood again like a man possessed.

I heard (there were three trying to pull me down) a head crack like a nut, and a sob or two as men choked in the stream. Then a hand clutched my collar and dragged me over a horse's hindquarters. "Hold by my middle," said a voice, "till we find deep water."

I did as I was bid, and but for a pike wound in my left thigh I came scatheless over the stream, and found that my horse had already swum to shore. As I crawled into the saddle again I saw my Captain, pistol in hand, shouting taunts to the Irishry who still swarmed in the water. Then came a yell of dismay, and the insurgents scattered everywhither, while our troop, whom they took to be the vanguard of an army, clattered down the hill. At this the Captain changed his shouts into a roar of laughter.

"Saw you ever such a man?" he cried. "There lives not the like of the Seneschal of Imokelly. He has no more than twenty men to our one, and lo! He is running like a hare. I owe him somewhat for the scratch on your leg, Mr Luttrell. Rest assured I will pay it. He will yet swing beside his yellow-faced Walloons, for such a cur deserves no gentleman's death."

After this spirited encounter we rode on to the city of Cork, where Captain Raleigh was closeted with my lord Grey of Wilton, while I sat in the common room of the Castle, with a bandaged leg, finding such entertainment from the converse of the officers of the Lord Deputy. Their chief tales were of this Captain of mine, about whom I was still in a divided humour. He had saved my life, 'twas true, but his courtesy was as a bone cast to a dog, a thing on which he seemed to set small value. There was ever in his eye that look of seeing me as smaller than God made me and I deemed myself. And yet at other times there flowed from him a merriment and a good fellowship which drew me to the man as he were my own brother.

In five days' time I was bidden attend my Captain on a journey to the West. We took fifty men of our foot-bank, for 'twas a mission of espionage and enquiry, in which we might fight or treat according to the humour of the rebels. Never have I seen a more sad and miry land. Two days we rode up the vale of a marshy stream, avoiding the morasses by endangering our necks on a rocky hillside. 'Twas the forefront of Spring, when in my native shire of Somerset the meads are bright with cuckoo-buds and cowslips, and every coppice is sweet with violets. But here there was nothing but a brown desert, where nesting moor-birds wailed dismally like the spirits of the lost. There were few inhabitants, and the huts of such as we saw were worse than an English sty. Now and then we would reach a fortalice, and some Irish lord would descend to greet us, with as like as not a dozen of our own soldiery quartered on him to devour his substance. I liked little the shifty wild eyes of the Irish; and as for their speech it was hid from me, for when they spoke our tongue 'twas with a mad roundabout twist in it. All the while the Captain would ride at the head of us, I at his side, and his mind very far from those weary deserts. Sometimes he would hum little snatches of song, and at other times he would be sunk in a contemplation from which I did not dare to summon him. As wayside company I have seen his better, but my liking for him advanced during those silent stages. There was in his air something secret and potent and masterful, and I resolved that if he were not a man to love he was assuredly a man to follow.

On the third day from Cork we came over a high ridge of mountain, and descended into a very lovely vale, which ran out to the Western Ocean. Here at length were we privileged to meet the Spring, for the fields and bushes were green and quickening, and every thicket was a cage of singing birds. At the foot we came to a narrow bay of salt water, which the Irish name a "lough," and riding by its side reached the castle of Kilmorice. The sentinel who challenged us told us that the land was quiet, and that Sir Thomas Astley had gone west to treat with the Chiefs of Desmond.

Indoors we found but one officer of the guard, the others having gone west with Sir Thomas. But in the great stone hall was seated a slim young man, who at the sight of us cried out and ran forward. I have rarely seen a face so transfigured as was my Captain's. The high and half-scornful demeanour vanished like ice in thaw. He clasped the young man in his arms and kissed him on both cheeks. "The sight of thee, old friend," he cried, "were worth a century of Irish journeys!"

The young man, I heard, was Master Edmund Spenser, a clerk of Cambridge, and chief secretary to my lord Grey of Wilton. He had a pale face and great brown eyes, which, in contrast with the alert gaze of a soldier, seemed drowsy and dreamy. He was most courteous in his conduct, offering us all manner of refreshment, and holding my Captain's hand as if he feared to lose him. Now I had been but a week in Captain Raleigh's service, but such was his power that his manifest love of Master Spenser provoked me to an extreme jealousy. I would have given my soul to have had my Captain's face glow thus at the sight of me.

As we sat in the hall after meat, with the rumour of the sea around us, Master Spenser fell into doleful mood. He lamented the sorrows of the Irish land, and the sad barbarities of war. Likewise he reproached his friend for his violence. The sack of Smerwick, of which he had been witness, still burned in his brain. " 'Twas not war, Walter," he cried; " 'twas a naked shambles. What profits our knightlihood if at the touch of wrath we become ravening beasts?"

My Captain replied very gently: "Nay, Edmund, I have no shame of Smerwick in my soul. Death, violent death is always a harsh sight; but if there be justice in it, it may take on the fairness of duty done. When I think of Smerwick I think of bloodier shambles to which the men who died there had aforetime condemned the innocent."

"But they died unarmed and in cold blood," said Master Spenser.

"So does the murderer on the gallows. And murderers and gallow-birds they were, every man of them. I blame my lord Grey for one thing only. He held the officers to ransom instead of sending them the way of their men. Mind you, they held no commission. They came out of the Pope's prisons and the darkest holes of Spain to make war without cause in this wretched land. That foul priest, Nicholas Saunders, was their fugleman; and their leaders were miscreants whom Europe had long ago cast forth. What treatment, think you, did they mete out to the English ships they took – ships out of my own Devon? What pity had they on the prisoners at Dingle? Have you heard how they used Youghal when they took the town, and slit every child's nose, and gouged out women's eyes, and slew every male thing? There is a long tally to count, and that morn at Smerwick went but a little way to the reckoning. When the Pope's vermin creep out of their dark haunts there is but one way to serve them. Let God's good light into their souls, though it be by steel and bullet."

Captain Raleigh's face had turned grim as death, and Master Spenser seemed to shrink from him. He saw movement, and, stretching his arm, clasped his friend's hand.

"You think me a fiery Protestant, Ned? But indeed I have cause and good reason. Did I not watch all through the night of Saint Bartholomew, when Queen Catherine and her Guises slaughtered those of the Reformed faith? That night I saw the gutters of Paris run with the noblest blood of France. I saw priests swollen with the lusts of hell urging on the spawn of the kennels to their accursed work, and crying the meek name of Christ as the warrant. I saw the shadow of an uplifted Cross lie athwart those scenes of death. And I swore by the living God that I, Walter Raleigh, should do what in me lay to root out of the earth this evil thing called Rome. The Pope is my foe, and after him his son of Spain, and till my right arm wither I shall strike at the cruel mummery of Rome and the blind tyranny of the Spaniard."

Master Spenser shook his head. "You have the fury in your bones," he said. "I mind when first I knew you, you told a tale of your mother's about a woman who suffered for her faith at Exeter Castle in Queen Mary's days, and you could scarce speak for tears. But, Walter, I would not reprove you for your religion. Heaven be my witness, that I love a man who will strike for his faith. But if you war against horrid cruelty and arrogance, I would have you war with a Christian reasonableness, not forgetting the ensample of the great Captain of our Salvation."

I had seen my master in many moods, but now I saw him in the strangest of all. There came into his face a gravity and a weight of reflection, the extreme opposite of his usual pride or his boyish merriment. 'Twas the face of one who thinks high thoughts and sees far horizons.

"I would remember," he said, "our great Ensample; but I conceive that if our Master be the Prince of Peace, He is no less the God of Battles. We of England, as I read the times, stand at the turn of our destiny. There is about us a black old world of ignorance and terror, where men's souls are enslaved to priests and their bodies to tyrants. We English stand for freedom and God's sunlight, and there can be no truce between us and the enemy. I take my motto from Holy Scripture: 'We wrestle not against flesh and blood, but against principalities, against powers, against the rulers of the darkness of this world'!"

But Master Spenser still shook his head in doubt.

"Nay, lad," said Raleigh, "I do not ask you to follow me. You are a poet, who sees a rosy world of his own creating, and by his skill makes of this drab earth in time something akin to his fancy. I am the plain man, who must dig and delve and make crooked things straight. In the end," he said, laughing in his subtle way, "we may reach the same goal, and by God's grace I may win some of the happiness of the poet."

That day, as it chanced, was the last I was to spend at ease for many months, since next morn we were summoned northward to the wars. Of my wounds and captivity I shall tell later, as also of my Captain's notable gallantry and excellent generalship. But on this afternoon I had, I think, a clearer sight of his great heart than I was ever to get thereafter. I had swayed between admiration and dislike. I had seen him as a mad boy, as a proud courtier, and as a sage statesman. Now I was to see him as a friend, and there was nothing under the vault of heaven more entrancing than the friendship of Walter Raleigh.

It had rained at midday, but in the evening the sky cleared, and my Captain bade me accompany him abroad to take the air, while Master Spenser sat indoors at his despatches. We ascended a rough hillside to a kind of table-land, and walked westward to where a great cliff broke down to the sea. 'Twas a bright evening, with fresh, clear airs blowing, and the whole sky ablaze with gold and crimson. He linked his arm in mine as we walked on the turf, with the sunset in our eyes, and he discoursed to me of my youth and my fortunes.

There are hours which are landmarks in a man's course, and which, in the retrospect, stand out like shining hilltops above the desert of his common occupations. Such was this hour to me; for it gave me the friendship of the greatest man I ever knew, and likewise a new purpose in life. Captain Raleigh talked little, but there flowed from the man that influence which is more persuasive than any words. The mere grasp of his arm was a power to convert a multitude.

By and by we stood on the sea-cliff, looking over a golden sea, with a dying sun making a path of crimson across the waters.

"I spoke of warring with Spain," said he, "but 'tis not in Europe that we will vanquish her. Graft this on your mind, Gervase, lad: the battlefront of our faith is gone from the Old World."

I am dull of understanding, and asked "Whither?"

"To the New World," he said. "The wars to come will be fought in the West. It is there that we of England can wreck King Philip and checkmate the Pope. Man, man, can you not see? We must have an Indies of our own: a New World to set against theirs. We must have wealth like Spain's, and a land to try the mettle of our youth. Give me that, and Europe is less to me than a pinch of dust."

He walked a few paces by himself to the extreme edge of the cliffs, and I waited behind, perceiving that he desired solitude. There he stood for maybe half an hour, watching the sun sink lower in the great ocean. There was a golden light on his hair and beard, and his figure on that headland was like some god of old romance. Then he turned to me, and in the twilight I could see that his eyes were once again light and wild, like a boy's.

"We are fools, Gervase, fools!" he cried. "Why do we abide in this dull land, making war on peasants, when there is the sea, the sea? We are no landsmen, we English. We fight best on the water... I have tried both warfares, and give me the salt air and the bellying of full sails, and the crash of timber and the clink of clean steel! A plague on a soldier's duties! If Brother Humphrey and his tall ships were in the bay there, I think I would cast duty to the winds. Get the West into your heart and blood, lad. 'Tis the goal of all English hopes."

Then he drew his sword, and statelily saluted the dying sun.

"*Addio*," he cried. "Another day we will follow your path, old friend."

By this time the dusk was falling grey. His face had grown stern again, as he turned to take my arm.

"Let us return for a little longer to our moorland wars," he said.

---

1 Written down by Gervase Luttrell, soldier of fortune, during the convalescence after wounds received in the Low Countries. The manuscript was given by him to the fellow-campaigner, Neill Macintyre of Glenbreac, in Argyll, among whose family papers it may still be read.

CHAPTER 3

Belphoebe's Smile [1]
(1587)

"To the heart of youth the world is a highwayside.
 Passing for ever, he fares; and on either hand,
 Deep in the gardens golden pavilions hide,
 Nestle in orchard bloom, and far on the level land
 Call him with lighted lamp in the eventide."

R L STEVENSON

...Edmund Spenser, my friend and master, has made a sweet tale of those whom he calls Belphoebe and Timias, by which names he signifies the Queen's excellent majesty and her knight, Walter Raleigh. The tale I now tell concerns both high personages at a great moment. Its stage is a greensward and a palace; the other players are the maids and gentlemen of Belphoebe's court; and the scenes are moved by the Loves and Destinies.

On Midsummer Day of the year 1587 the Court lay at Ashridge, the great house by Berkhampstead, in the shire of Hertford. Thither I came in the train of my lord Burghley, for he needed a scholar by his side, being himself unhandy with the pen. Her Majesty the Queen Gloriana, as the wits named her, had ridden from Windsor, and was busy with her maids in the ordering of a

Midsummer masque. This noble lady had aforetime been gracious in her notice of me, and the last summer, in her progress through my own shire of Sussex, I had been favoured to lead the revels with her at Battle. I looked now for some share in the sunshine of her regard, but found that a greater had forestalled me. For with the Court was Sir Walter Raleigh, whose light had dimmed my lord Leicester's, and for the moment shone brightest in the sky of fashion. Some years before he had returned from the Irish wars, and had been given great lands and offices, so that his state far outran the modesty of a private gentleman. There was none so high, not even my lord Burghley, who did not seek his favour. He had sent forth fleets to the Indies, and had created a new England in the West, which he named *Virginia* in his mistress' praise. Likewise in Ireland he played the part of merchant adventurer, and had made of his estates an English plantation. I liked the man little, but I was overborne by his magnificence. 'Twas not riches or power alone, but poetry and learning that he sought. He was the friend of all scholars, and in the Mermaid Tavern in Bread Street held symposia, where all who loved the Muses found fair fellowship. To his lodgings by the river in the palace of the Lord Bishop of Durham trooped the wits of England. Once and again I had been privileged to join them, and found sage divines side by side with playwrights, and all held captive by their host's address. Two years before, indeed, I had supped with him, and listened till cock-crow while he discussed divine philosophy with the lamented Sir Philip Sidney and an Italian, by name Giordano Bruno, who was little admired by the devout. As I say, I liked him not, but all men love to watch the transit of a bright star. So I watched from my humble coign, and was not ashamed to find my eyes dazzle.

My little masque – 'twas a thing about Flora and the Hours – was graciously accepted by the Queen, who said 'twould do as well as another for her maids to show their pretty ankles in. But as I walked in the herb garden I fell in with Sir Walter, whose memory held my face. Said he, "Your plaything lacks salt, Sir Gabriel. 'Tis dainty as madrigal, but sugar cloys. Your nymphs are but silken wenches, and no daughters of Themis and the king of gods."

His manner ruffled me, and I answered that a masque was in essence a silken thing. "Would you have me set a dance of Amazons?" I asked.

"Nay, little poet," he said, pinching my ear in his mocking fashion. "But a thing may be fine and yet hard as adamant. The slim goddess may wield the lightnings. Regard my blade," he says, letting his sword slip half out of its sheath. "It bends like whipcord, it sings like a lute, and yet 'twill split a skull if rightly wielded. And this arm of mine is no branch of oak, but I wager 'twould keep its own against the lustiest smith's. There Sir Gabriel, I give you a theme for a sonnet. You may call it 'Strength not in Bulk but in Spirit,' and sing it to an Italian air."

We strolled past the sundial and out of the yew portal, while I fumed with wrath at the man's presumption. 'Twas the truth that stung me; for I knew in my heart that my Hours were but silk and cambrick, things neither divine nor human. Now from so high a wit as Raleigh I would have taken reproof gladly, had his air been otherwise. But he treated my craft as it had been a child's whim. The next moment, indeed, he had forgotten that he had spoken, and was twitching the lillies' heads with his ivory wand and humming a little tune. I looked sideways at him as we walked, and marked the insolent grace of his form and the noble poise of his head. He walked with the freest carriage I have ever seen in a man, as if he were indeed lord of life and the world his humble minister.

On the pleasaunce we found Her Majesty with her maids and a dozen gentlemen of the Court, seated in a green spot shaded by beeches. The Queen was working embroidery, and capping verses with young Master Trefusis, who lay at her feet. As we neared, she cried out to me and bade us to join the circle. I awaited by the edge of the group, but Sir Walter sate himself by the Queen's side next to a tall fair maid, Mistress Elizabeth Throckmorton, who welcomed him shyly with a smile. Gloriana noted the greeting, and frowned.

"We speak of love, my Raleigh," she said, with an acid in her voice. "Here we are all equipped for a pastoral, singing like shepherdesses of the Golden Age. Master Treyfusis has been inditing a doleful ballad to my Bess' eyebrows. See if you can better it. Speak it, Master Trefusis."

The boy blushed hotly. "An your Majesty please, 'twas not my own. 'Twas a song of Kit Marlowe's that he called 'The Passionate Shepherd to his Love.' If it be your will, I will repeat it."

He declaimed in a dulcet voice a pretty poem in which a shepherd bribes his lady with the joys of a country life. The maids clapped their hands.

"Better it, Sir Walter," said the Queen.

"Nay, Madam, give me a minute's grace, and I will write the lady's answer," he said.

He plucked forth his tablets and wrote for a little while. Gloriana's hands were busy with her stitches.

"What a housewife I am!" she cried. "I have not wrought so hard since as a child, in this very place, I made baby clothes for Mary, my royal sister. Some day I will show them to you. Delicate work, I vow, and as quaint a bribe as sisterly fear ever devised for sisterly whimsies. *Ay de mi!* The gift and its cause alike came to little. How now, Sir Walter? Is you response complete?"

Raleigh lifted his head, and looking now at the Queen and now at Mistress Throckmorton, read his verses:

> "If all the world and love were young,
> And truth in every shepherd's tongue,
> These pretty pleasures might me move
> To live with thee and be thy Love.
>
> But Time drives flocks from field to fold;
> When rivers rage and rocks grow cold;
> And Philomel becometh dumb;
> The rest complains of cares to come.
> The flowers do fade, and wanton fields

To wayward Winter reckoning yields:
A honey tongue, a heart of gall,
Is fancy's spring, but sorrow's fall.

Thy gowns, thy shoes, thy beds of roses,
Thy cap, thy kirtle, and thy posies,
Soon break, soon wither – soon forgotten,
In folly ripe, in reason rotten.

Thy belt of straw and ivy buds,
Thy coral clasps and amber studs, –
All these in me no means can move
To come to thee and be thy Love.

But could youth last, and love still breed,
Had joys no date, nor age no need,
Then these delights my mind might move
To live with thee and be thy Love"

They were delicate verses, as far beyond the skill of us common bards as Sir Walter's magnificence was beyond our modesty. I think, if Apollo had given me so great a gift, I would have been content to forswear Courts for ever and seek a hermitage.

Gloriana laughed loud. "A shrewd retort, i' faith! Our Raleigh is but a laggard lover. Had he been a maid, there would have been broken hearts among the men. How now, Bess?" She said, turning to Mistress Throckmorton. "Does Sir Walter interpret aright the hearts of us virgins?"

The maid looked up, blushing. "Nay, Madam, an it please you, I think he would make us too crafty. He forgets that love is blind and laughs at precepts."

"Ay, wench, you are in the right of it. 'Tis the way of men. They call us coy and cold, but 'tis they who are the pedlars and hucksters of love. 'Tis we women alone who will abandon all to the God and count no consequences."

Sir Walter said nothing, but a subtle smile lurked in the corners of his mouth. He looked at the Queen, and she met his eyes squarely, but not for long. Soon she dropped her gaze, and, if I be not blind, there was no less than a blush on her august cheek. I think her mind had flown to my lord Leicester and others whom she had used ill.

Presently, with many bowings and excuses, Master Askew appeared, the master of the pageant that was to be given at sundown, and begged for the attention of his players. The Queen shooed them away like a flock of geese. "Get you to your mumming, children," she cried; "Sir Walter and I have matters of high statecraft to discourse on. Get you gone, I say."

I would have departed with the others; but she motioned me imperiously to bide. "Wait with us, Sir Poet. I would have you stay, for Sir Walter and I are prone to quarrel, and need a peacemaker."

I think she had detected my dislike of Raleigh, and desired me to remain that my presence might humble him. For as soon as we were alone she began to rate him furiously. There was that in our lady Gloriana's colour and mien which in her anger made her a very Fury of wrath.

"So ho, my fair Sir Walter," she says, "you are the coy Sir Galahad in your verse, but I catch you forever making eyes at Bess Throckmorton."

Raleigh had arisen and was standing by a beech trunk, his cape of purple Cyprus velvet hanging low on his arm.

"Nay, Madam," he said; "you wrong me. I have remarked the lady that she is kind and fair, but I have eyes for no woman but the Queen of England."

"Idle words," said Gloriana scornfully. "You swear your devotion, but a pretty wench breaks all your vows. 'Tis the way of mankind, from Kings and Emperors to the last lout of a country boy I have plucked out of Devon mud and made a man o'. Think you a mother loves to see her brood ensnared by wiles of other females? There never yet was a woman who hated not in her heart her son's wife. Think you I am so free from the common emotions of my sex that I can suffer gladly to see my cavaliers, vowed for service to me alone, dancing like apes in the train of misses whose mothers but yesterday bound up their hair?"

Raleigh had narrowed his eyes to slits, and was listening gravely. Had he smiled, I think his life would have paid for his folly, but he was ever one to know to a nicety the limits of daring. I stood apart, most grievously ill at ease, wishing that Her Majesty would bid me to join the mummers.

"Speak, you wooden doll!" cried the Queen, her cheek flaming scarlet.

"What shall I say, Madam?" Sir Walter answered in a low, soft voice. "Your Majesty's care of your servants is more tender than any mother's yet we look not to you as a mother. You are the greatest of earthly Queens, yet we look not up to you as Queen. For your Majesty is above all things woman, and on woman a man must look squarely, neither up nor down. In the Kingdom of Hearts the worshipper and the worshipped are on level ground."

There was a bold speech for you! He spoke with such a gentle and grave assurance that the Queen's eyes dropped. 'Twas but for a moment. She fired again, and cried out in a voice harsh as a man's: "By Harry's soul, you Devon sprigs have more conceit than any Spaniard! You are likewise heretics, and would proclaim the Queen of England mere woman, against the teaching of his Grace of Canterbury and his Right Reverence of London. Hoity toity! Some of you will cool your heels in the Tower for this." But she laughed all the while, and tapped her little feet on the greensward, so that her needles and embroidery spilled on the lawn.

Presently she looked up at Raleigh, archly as a maid in her teens looks on a lover. And this was Gloriana, who had left her teens those thirty years and more. I dare not say that she was old. There are women – and men likewise – of so great a zest for life that the body seems to keep pace with the spirit. Certain the Queen of England had the power at moments to look as young and fair as the ageless Queen of Love. 'Twas when the spirit failed her that her cheeks pinched, her brow lined, and her eye grew dull.

"Is there man bold enough," she asked in a honeyed voice, "to see behind the Queen to the woman? You lack not courage, Sir Walter."

'Twas a strange scene, and one I would have given a thousand crowns to be quit of. I think that both must have forgotten my presence. For if ever there was wooing in a tone, 'twas in the Queen's. The flush of youth sat on her cheek, and her eyes sparkled like a shallow in Spring. One delicate hand played with an Italian greyhound crouched at her feet, the other tapped restlessly on her knees. She was looking at Sir Walter from under lowered lids.

He knelt before her and kissed her hand.

"I speak," he said, "what all men know. Your Majesty has long held the hearts of your cavaliers in the hollow of this little hand. To me you are neither Queen nor mother, but goddess, the lady of love and dawn. You have but one rival in my heart."

"A rival!" The words were hissed between her teeth. The hand was snatched away and the eyelids opened, like a curtain drawn from a window to reveal without a storm of lightnings. But Sir Walter looked up unmoved.

"Ay, Madam, and that rival is your own surpassing greatness. For if you are lady to love, you are goddess to serve. 'Twas you who gave to us all our warrant of chivalry and sent us out on the King's Path. We cannot draw back even at your bidding. We have your commands to do this and do that for your realm of England; and seeing that you are England, 'tis for you we labour. Think it not unkind that the love of your servants is merged in worship. 'Tis but the deeper for that, though it lack common expression."

The Queen spoke hoarsely. "Your words are riddles, sir, like a priest's," she said.

Raleigh stood up, so that he towered over her slim sitting form.

"Not riddles but parables. There are some who are cast for so high a destiny that they must forswear homely joys. 'Tis not that they lack the plain affections, but that they possess the greater

34

duties. Such is the Queen of England, who fights God's battles against an armed world. Such in a little way is her lowly servant, Walter Raleigh, who fights 'neath her banner. To him she is the goddess, queen, and mistress, but being Queen, her royalty demands service before love."

Gloriana looked up at last.

"Then for us poor Queens there is no love," she said, and her voice was thick as if she spoke through tears.

"Nor for us poor knights," said he. "You are playing with the world's fates, Madam. For you there is the love of God and of your people and of the unborn generations that will arise in your England and call you blessed. But there is no room for common love. You are beyond man's reach, and you have set your knights on the same stony steeps of honour."

Once again fell a silence.

Then, without lifting her head, the Queen spoke. "I thank you, my lord. You have spoken honestly and bravely, as a true man should. I pray you to go now and bid my maids attend me."

I noted that she called him "my lord." I think her mind was harking back to a day when she and my lord Leicester had spoken of the same matter. We of the Court had guessed often at the conclusion, but now I learnt the truth; save that I think that the words now spoken by Raleigh had been in the Queen's mouth.

I spent the day in a deep perplexity; and late in the afternoon sought out Sir Walter Raleigh when he was walking on the great terrace above the fish-ponds. I reminded him of the morning, and offered myself for the duello.

"I place my life in your hand," said I. "God knows I have never loved you, but I am man enough to appraise your manhood. This morn I was the unwilling spectator at a scene which deeply concerns my mistress' honour and your own. 'Tis for you to say whether one who has seen what I have seen can be suffered to live. I take the chance of death at your hands."

I had looked for his acceptance, or perchance some cold and scornful rejoinder which would have goaded me to insult. Instead, he laid both hands on my shoulders, and there were tears in his eyes.

"Kill you, Sir Gabriel! By my faith, 'twould be to make the world too poor. You ask me to do murder upon one whose sole offence is that he has over nice a sense of honour. Fight you, forsooth! I would liefer embrace you."

He twined his arm in mine and drew me beyond the terrace into the hollows of the great park. When a man is strung up to a desperate resolve he is in no mood for pleasantry, and I would have stayed his going had I not seen that in his face which constrained me. 'Twas the face of one who had passed through a deeper perplexity than mine, and was still in the throes of it. The high light air, the pride, the brave deportment, had gone, and in their place left a much-vexed, deep-thinking man. The courtier was unmasked.

Down in a thicket of green bracken a herd of deer was feeding. The scene after twenty years stands as clear in my mind as if it had been yesterday. There came a faint noise of lutes and viols from the terrace, where the mummers were ordering the pageant. A country wench in a yellow gown was singing as she took the track to Berkhampstead. Up in the beechen shade cushats were crooning, and a low hum of bees filled the sweet-scented air. 'Twas a very Arcadia of summer loveliness, and there in the midst of it stood we two perplexed mortals, wrinkling our brows at Fate.

Raleigh flung himself on the greensward and plucked idly at a flower.

"I wish to Heaven I had a pipe of tobacco," he said. "The herb is a sovran cure for ill temper. You have heard and seen, Sir Gabriel. Perchance you now know somewhat of the trials of us poor favourites of Fortune. There lives no greater soul under God than this Queen of ours, but she is very woman, and her womanhood is the burden which beats down the wings of her greatness. She has created such a Round Table as King Arthur never dreamed of, but she is reluctant to send out her knights on their missions."

I had nought to say, but could only watch the moody face of this splendid gentleman, who thus confessed his heart.

"All the world envies me," he went on. "I have been honoured with Her Majesty's special favour. I have been given estates and high offices. My substance is great, and my degree and honour of the noblest. But what profits it, man? I am still a captive, in fetters of fine silk and pure gold. By my faith, a tarry sailor in a Bristol barque has more of a man's task than mine."

"You have the ordering of high places of state," I ventured.

"Places of state!" he laughed. "Ay, old Burghley comes with his ferret face and begs my consideration. But what of that? I am as little of a statesman as Her Majesty's favourite lady. I open the way to her presence. Perchance my advice is asked, but my words weigh nothing. The Queen loves my blunt speech, but she hearkens only to her tame fox, and to herself."

He got to his feet and strode up and down.

"Mark you, Sir Gabriel, I have but the one passion, to make this good England the sun of all the world. I see her enemies clustering around as thick as locusts. I see such a breed of men within our shores as would, if unchained, sweep land and sea clear of our ill-wishers. I see a great-hearted and most wise lady, who loves her people well, but, womanlike, will tarry, and in her tenderness to youth will clip its wings. She suffers me to send my expeditions to the Indies, but laughs at them as if they were a merry whim. For myself, she forbids me to leave these shores, and well I know that where no leader is there will be no glory. I strut peacock-like about the Court, petted, flattered, envied; but before God I would rather have a tall ship and a Devon crew, and be risking my all on a desperate enterprise. A Court is nothing but a green-sickness for a man's spirit."

Then he approached me and laid his hands again on my shoulders.

"Pardon me, fair friend, if I spoke slightingly of that life to which you are vowed. There are honest men whose light shines best in such a scene of leisure and peace. Would that Edmund Spenser would join you in this world of gardens and indite his divine measures in your good company! But for me, I am another fibre. A brown moor-cock is ill at ease among the doves and peacocks of a pleasaunce. I have no gift for Courts. I like little their soft beds, and rich dress and dainty foods. I would rather the smell of salt than the scent of musk. Nay, I had rather the sour Irish mosses than this Arcady. For I am a man who must be up and doing or he stifles. I know the gifts God has given me. I can lead rough fellows up to the cannon's mouth; and I think I have a native genius for seacraft. I will search you out the riches of strange lands, for the love of them burns in me. But for this philandering and dancing and versifying, my soul loathes it! Good my friend, I speak to you honestly as to a true man. Some day the silken cords will be cut, and the world will mark the fall of Raleigh. But haply Raleigh will be gone on a better business."

His voice stopped suddenly, and the grave passion vanished from his face. In its stead came the look of railing gallantry which was his Court manner. I glanced behind and saw the cause.

A very pretty lady came tripping over the sward.

"Sweet sir," she lisped, "I am bidden fetch you. Master Askew hath need of you. The Masque begins in another hour, and the advice of Sir Gabriel is sought on certain high matters. Master Askew would consult, too, with Sir Walter touching his raiment. It is thought the white taffeta sown with black pearls would be fitting garb for the King of the Shades..."

---

1 From the papers of Sir Gabriel Bretton, poet, playwright, and Knight of the Shire for Sussex. Sir Gabriel also left an MS play on the subject, entitled *Gloriana, or The Courtier Unmask'd*.

CHAPTER 4

Manoa the Golden 1
(1595)

"O watchman, leaning from the mast,
    What of the night? The shadows flee,
The stars grow pale, the storm is past,
    A blood-red sunrise stains the sea.
At length, at length, O desperate wills,
    Luck takes the tiller and foul tides turn;
Superb amid majestic hills
    The domes of Eldorado burn."
The Ship of Fools

...My head was buzzing like a spinning-top, and it seemed that scalding water fell on me so that I could scarce draw breath. Also there was an orange-tawny bird, with a blue beak and a face like the parsons of Budleigh, that kept cocking a wicked eye on me and flapping his wings. I besought Amias Thyn to kill the fowl, but he answered that 'twas only a fancy of my fever. Upon that I up and fetched Amias a blow on the face, and myself the next moment toppled to the earth. For certain I was very near my end. The poison from the arrow-head had wrought desperately in my blood, and I was fallen into the last fever of the brain.

39

I was now five months out of England, weary months in truth for body and soul. Since the February morn when we sailed from Plymouth, we had traversed many thousand leagues of ocean, made capture of ships, and laid hands on the new-built Spanish city of Saint Joseph in the isle of Trinidad. For guide we had Captain Jacob Whiddon, an old voyager in these parts, and for fellow-adventurers young bloods from every manor in the West, and likewise some tough and salted sea-captains to correct the yeast of youth. Our Admiral was that famous knight Walter Raleigh, the Captain of Her Majesty's Guard, and the Lieutenant-General of the County of Cornwall. Aforetime I had known this Sir Walter, when he was the glory and particular star of the Court. He was used to come among us of the sea at every port in the West, and would sit for hours discussing of our travels. I have seen him at Falmouth and Plymouth, in rich robes and chains of gold, seated hard by a tarry sailorman, as if he had never trod softer floors than a ship's deck. Hence he was vehemently beloved by all seafarers, but he had ever a moody brow and a dark eye, save when he glowed at some tale of adventure. We had heard how he had fallen into disgrace with the Queen, and was enclosed for long in the Tower of London, and then banished to his country manor. When the word went round that he was equipping a fleet for a venture to the Indies, there was no man from Southampton to Bristol but burned to sail with him. I mind well how he came down to Plymouth Quay to join his ships, with so gay a step and light an eye you would have thought him no more than boy. When the crews cheered him from the bulwarks, he waved his hat and smiled like a man who has at last come home.

But to my tale. From Trinidad we set out in a flotilla, for our vessels could not ascend the river Orinoko, because of the shoals and currents. The whole company of us had to ship in three wherries and a barge. As for the Admiral, he had an old gallego boat cut down so that she drew but five feet of water, fitted her with banks of oars, and embarked in her with sixty officers and gentlemen-volunteers. After that I mind little save the sickness that racked us in the open sea ere we made the mouth of the river, and the perilous water-ways we laboured through thereafter. There was no room to land, for the woods came down to the edge as thick as furze and reached evil claws into the water. The air was full of fever, and the heat of the sun like gusts from a baker's oven. We were for ever grounding in shallows, and to shove off had to wade deep in the stream, in mortal fear of the noisome toothed serpents called Lagartos that dwell in such rivers. From ill feeding and unchanged raiment we became foul and offensive alike to our fellows and ourselves; and the incessant toil of rowing, in which gentle and simple shared alike, came near to driving us mad. But through it all the Admiral abated nothing of his courage and sweet temper. He would urge us on with a cheerful word and a merry quip, and the weakest would bend stoutly to the oars if he saw Sir Walter near him.

Presently we came out of the narrows to the main stream of the Orinoko, and found the noblest country mine eyes had ever beheld. 'Twas a great park, full of green grass and high groves of trees and a multitude of fruits. The deer flocked to the water's edge as if they had been used to a keeper's call. Now 'twas possible to land, and eat and sleep on solid ground. A merry wind sprang up behind us and lessened the toil of rowing, and, having abundant food and good knowledge of the way, our hearts were wondrously uplifted. On the seventh day we saw afar off toward the West a blue line of mountains and rejoiced, for we knew them for the husk of El Dorado.

After a fortnight's passage, during which we saw many curious things, we came to Morequito, the port of the kingdom of Aromaia, and found there the King Topiawari, whose nephew had been foully slain by the Spaniard. He welcomed us graciously, and gave us bread and wine and all manner of flesh and fowl; likewise a quantity of pine-apples, the princess of all fruits, which purgeth the fever from a man's blood. As the King led us about his country we remarked the rocks streaked with gold, which was no Marquesite, such as appears in other parts of the Indies, but the true "Mother of Gold" that is the guide to rich metal below the soil. Also we found a stone like a sapphire, and the people had great wealth of spleen-stones, or, as some name them, emeralds. But especially the King Topiawari told the Admiral of the City of Manoa, where the Incas rule, which lieth many leagues west by south in the high hills. All round the base of the mountain dwelleth a fierce tribe, by name the Epimureans, who are in league with the Inca and keep his marches. They war with the other Indian peoples, and the King was earnest with us to join him in a march against them. But the Admiral considered that we had too few men for such a venture, and that the floods of the river which were now beginning made it impolitic to penetrate further that year in the direction of Manoa. He therefore resolved to return, being satisfied of the great riches of the country and the friendly disposition of the people to our mistress the Queen of England. The Indians marvelled at our clemency and justice, for by the Admiral's orders no man might take so much as a potato plant from one of the poor people without making him satisfaction.

'Twas in the last days of June that my troubles began. The Admiral sent for me and told me his purpose of return. He said that he desired more knowledge about the golden parts of Guiana, and the civil towns and apparelled people of the Incas, and he desired this knowledge from English eyes and lips. There was an old Cacique, dwelling in the upper vales of the Caroni, a river of Aromaia, whose town was but two days' march from the borders of the Epimureans. He was willing to guide me to the borders, if haply from some hill-top I might get sight of the great lake on which stands the City of Manoa. Then he would lead me back by a shorter path, so that I might join the flotilla on its homeward journey. "You will take with you Amias Thyn," said Sir Walter, "for I can spare no more English. And God be with you, Nathan, for I know you a man of discretion and good heart."

By this time I was somewhat restored in health, and my eagerness for the errand had almost made me leap with joy. We departed on a fine sunshine morning, and journeyed in boats as far as the flow of the Caroni allowed. But since the flood-time was beginning the rowers could scarcely win a stone's throw in an hour, so we put to land, and travelled on foot beyond the falls of the river, which are a dozen in number and each as high as a church tower. Thereafter we reached a country of short grass and pressed on easily, save that Amias Thyn, who was no footman, lagged somewhat behind. By the second evening we had come to the town of the Cacique, and were civilly lodged in a hut of wood. That night the people of the place brought us pineapple wine in stone jars, and so caroused with us that Amias was like to have perished of colic.

The next morn we set out with the Cacique and two Indian guides into the woods which stretched to the country of the Epimureans. From the start I knew that the venture was to be ill-fated, for I saw three crows on a single branch, and Amias, being giddy from the night's frolic, shot at one with his musket. The Cacique warned us that the woods were full of evil men, who are of a different race from the Indians and are called, I think, Aroras. They have squat bodies and sleek black hair, and live on human flesh. Also they shoot poisoned arrows, of which only the Indian soothsayers know the cure. But, said he, his tribe was at peace with the Aroras, and if we went discreetly and fast we might win through without trouble.

All went well till the afternoon of the next day, when we seemed to be near the edge of the trees, for in the gaps we could see peaks of mountains. We had halted for food, when there came a cry from the guide who led us and rustling in the thicket. Presently I saw a dark face among the leaves, and ere I knew something pierced my shoulder. I fired my musket at the invisible foe, and Amias did the like; and the next second all was quiet save for the mutterings of the Indians. But when the Cacique saw my wound he set up a great lamentation, and cried out that I had taken a deadly poison. A faintness fell on me, and in a dream I suffered him to cut away the flesh and burn the wound with powder. Then

I was dragged between the Indians at a great pace through the trees until we came to the edge of a rocky upland.

That Cacique was the best Christian it has ever been my lot to meet. He bade his men make a rough hut for me, in which I lay tortured with pain and yet so weak that I could scarce move to ease my anguish. He gave me medicine, but it seemed that he had not the knowledge of the royal cure. For he bade Amias watch me close to prevent me doing a mischief in my madness, and set off to find an Indian soothsayer who should heal my wound. All this Amias told me later…

So I come of where my tale began as I lay raving in the hut on the border of the Epimureans. After I smote Amias I lost all knowledge of the world. In such state I lay for hours, and then about the first light my mind cleared. The torture had gone, my wits had returned, but I felt the life ebbing in my members. I knew that death was near, and strove to turn my mind to thoughts of heaven. But all I could see was the blessed orange-tawny bird with the face of the parson of Budleigh.

I noted Amias sunk in sleep on the ground, as weary as a hound after the chase. I wanted to laugh at the oddity of his red face burrowed into the leaves. Then the screen of boughs was lifted and I saw the Cacique bending over me, and with him another. That other was an old man with a thin white beard and a high nose; and I thought him a white heron come to fight the terrible orange-tawny fowl.

I know not what he did to me, but six hours later I awoke from deep slumber with the pain gone and my health restored, save for a singing in my head like the fall of a weir. There was Amias smoking a pipe, and the Cacique and the old soothsayer playing a game on a thing like a chessboard.

"Ho, there!" I cried in a thin voice. "God has raised me up, and His name be praised! We have no time to tarry if I am to join the Admiral. We must be up and off this very day."

The priest came to my side. He was a lean old man, the gloom of his complexion grown by age to a fine ivory.

"What came you out for to seek?" he asks, like the Scriptures.

"I am bidden by the Admiral to find the hill in the land of the Epimureans from which a man may see the City of Manoa." I spoke in Spanish to the Cacique, who turned my words into the Indian tongue.

The old man shook his head. "I have heard of you English as a great people of the East, who worship the one God and are ruled by a Virgin. You do justly by all men, and rob not like those of Spain. But why seek you Manoa?"

"Why?" I cried. "Because of the tales of it. 'Tis a mystery that fires our blood. I want to see the princes who smear their bodies with gum and roll in gold dust, and the city so great that if a man enters one afternoon 'tis the evening of the next day ere he comes to the King's Palace. I would see the golden battlements, and the golden birds that sing by magic, and the golden flowers that deck the islands. I mind of a lame Spaniard in Cartagena who had a pouch full of gold beads that he told me were the pebbles of the lake shore."

"And if you win there, you English, what next?" says the priest.

"For us common folk there will be gold," said I. "I know not the mind of my Admiral, but 'tis rumoured that he would ally our kingdom with the Grand Inca, and make so strong a band against the Spaniard as to drive him forth of Tierra Firme."

The priest spoke in Indian to the Cacique. Then he looked first at me and then at Amias as if he would search our souls.

"My brother has sworn to lead you to the Hill of Vision," he said. "And it is just that he should keep truth. But I warn you that ill may come of it. The Golden City is strong guarded by the spells of dead kings. I cannot break them. No stranger from the East will fare better."

I answered that I feared no charm, being strong in the Christian faith; but he paid little heed to my words.

45

"You are feeble," he said, "and 'tis a hard journey. I have brought you back from the edge of death. Will you trust me to fortify you for travel?"

The Cacique was earnest with me to swallow the priest's drug; for without this, he said, we should both faint by the way. From a wallet he took some little packets and mingled two potions each, for me and Amias. The first was bitter as wormwood and set my ears drumming so that I feared deafness. The second put me into a great ease and contentment, so that I could have sung aloud for joy. Amias, who was ever a fool, did indeed sing – a tavern ditty about Poll and Sue, which he fitted to a melancholious psalm tune.

A little later we started, while it was still forenoon, and travelled up the rocky slope of the hills. The priest and I rode on mules which he had brought, while Amias and the Cacique went on foot. Amias was for ordinary a miserable footman, but the potion he had drunk so filled him with eagerness that he outstepped the mules. We spoke little, being deep sunk in peace. All I knew was that we mounted ever higher, till we saw the land behind us lie flat to the Orinoko, and in front and on either hand great swellings of mountain.

I mind the exceeding gladness I felt. 'Twas like boyhood returned, with no sin to burden the conscience and no failure to cloud the spirit. Whether 'twas the drug or the high air I know not, but I seemed to be out of the body. We wound up a track that led to a pass in the hills, and in the nick of it the sun was setting like an eye of fire. I made certain that beyond that pass lay Manoa: indeed the sky had a shimmer of light as if it had caught the reflection from acres of gold; and I cried on the others to hasten, that we might win up by nightfall. But the pass was longer than I had judged, and at the darkness we were forced to camp some way short of the summit.

I ate little food, and soon fell asleep in deep weariness. All night long I dreamed of angels and heavenly mansions, so delectable a dream that I could have wept at the wakening. 'Twas a clear dawn, and no man spoke as we saddled the mules and took our way toward the ridge of the mountains.

Many times in my life I have been a-quiver with eagerness, so that my knees loosened under me, and my heart smote on my ribs. I have felt thus in a sea-fight before the shots began, and very notably when I waited on Nell Ottaway's answer to the declaration of my love. But never in love or war have I felt so shattering a tremor. Even the muddy soul of Amias Thyn was kindled to expectation. Every step, I thought, would bring me the promised sight, but a ridge intervened, and still another. At last, when I did not look for it, we had turned a corner and stood on a ledge gazing on a new country.

I fell off my mule, and with Amias viewed the prospect on my knees, calling on God to be merciful to sinful men. For this was what I saw…

Below me the cliffs fell sheer for a mile or so to a plain of greenest grass where herds of white cattle grazed. There was a brimming river winding through the meadows, as I have seen the Thames wind in the fields by Richmond. Beyond these pastures were orchards, where it seemed to me I could see golden fruit hang as thick as haws on a whitethorn. And beyond the orchards was a lake, so long that to left and right its blue waters were lost in haze. On this lake I saw the white sails of many craft, and on its multitude of isles white towers and flowery gardens.

But beyond the lake was the sight that bankrupted me of breath and sent Amias to his prayers. For there stood a city so great and noble that it seemed as if no mortal could have raised it. 'Twas all of shimmering white like sea-foam, but the roofs were of naked gold. I saw the streets run in pleasant lines to a great palace set on a low hill, which was assuredly the jewel of so fair a casket. Its golden dome was like a mirror, in which the clouds showed themselves and the sun was re-born.

Yet 'twas not the riches and magnificence of Manoa that melted my heart: 'twas its air of happy peace. From my hill-top I could see no inhabitants, though a faint hum of life rose to my ears. But a kind of glory brooded there such as the Blessed may hope for in Paradise. I had forgotten about gold and fame, for the thing seemed too precious to pollute with mortal thoughts. 'Twas a realm so far more lovely and desirable than the greatest empire that I could scarce believe it to be of this world. As for Amias he did nothing but weep and pray.

"You see Manoa, my son," said the priest's voice. "If you would see your friends again, 'tis time to depart."

At this I fell into despair. I could not leave so noble a vision. I besought him to show me the entrance, though it should cost me years of travel. Nay, I would gladly have starved slowly on that ledge of rock so that I could have feasted my eyes on the City.

"There is no entrance for you," he said. "The folk of the City are wise, and would keep free from the wars and sorrows of the world. They have guarded their land with spells that no man can break save with their good will. I have brought you to the sight of it, because I have heard of the honour of your people. Think well of it, my son; 'tis not fitting to mar so fair a thing for any lust of treasure. Seek your gold mines elsewhere, for you cannot reach the pure gold of the City of the Sun."

I asked if no man had entered the place.

"Once," said he, "a man found the key after years of toil, but it profited him nothing. He entered the City and saw its glories, but his soul was earthy and the sight destroyed his wits. He was led forth, and travelled back to the Spanish towns, but he babbled wild things and died in a frenzy. No man believed his tale... But see. The Gods warn us. If we would save our lives, we must depart."

A black thundercloud was gathering round the heights, and in another minute the storm burst, almost sweeping us from our ledge. We hastened to leave, the regret in my soul so choking me that I had no speech, nor any strength to stay. But as we went I noted one marvel. For, whereas the storm was dark around us to the edge of the cliff, beyond 'twas clear sunlight. Through the

driving sleet I had one last glimpse of the shining towers of Manoa
the Golden...

Seven days later, on the bank of the Orinoko, we met with the
Admiral's flotilla. Seven weary days they proved, so that Amias
and I were but hollow-eyed scarecrows when out of the swamps
we hailed the first boats. We had both fallen into a fever, partly
from toil and partly from the regret and wonder of our minds.
Indeed 'twas little I cared what befell me. Ravening beasts and
savage men were as nothing compared with the ache of loss in my
heart.

Sir Walter had me aboard the gallego, and in presence of his
officers and volunteers questioned me on our adventure. I begged
that I might tell them first to his private ear; and seeing the
earnestness of my demeanour and the marks of labour I bore on
me, he granted my request. So that evening, when we had landed
on an isle to pass the night, he took me apart into a woody place
and asked for my tale.

I told him as well as I could of my wound in the forest, of its
cure, and the journey to the gap of the hills. Then I spoke of
Manoa so far as my poor words could envisage such a marvel. The
Admiral heard me with eager eyes.

"You saw it, my brave Nathan? But that is what no Spaniard
these fifty years hath done!"

"Ay, but I saw it from a mountain-top, and I saw no way to
enter."

"Cliffs can be scaled," said he; "and if there be another ingress,
it will be found. The great matter is that the City is there, and can
be viewed in two days' march into the land of the Epimureans. It
needs but a man skilled in travel to chart the valley, and discover
where the river you speak of leaves it. What the Spaniard Martinez
could do is not beyond the range of Englishmen."

Then he fell to questioning me about small particulars, being
very curious about the islands in the lake and the great white
palace or temple which commanded the City. He wrote down in
a book what I had to tell him, and made a chart of the place and

the way thereto. He was warm in his commendation. "When we return," he says, "you shall lead the advance, Nathan. As you were the first to see the City, so you shall be the first of the English to tread its streets."

"Your pardon, sir," said I, "but these same streets I will never tread."

And when he asked my meaning, I up and spoke what was in my heart.

"I am a man of blood and guile," I said, "whose life has been spent in pursuits the most conducing to these faults. But all the while I have a proper notion of virtue, and I would not sin against God's plain command. That City, I take it, is as Eden before our father Adam sinned. I know not whether the folk who dwell in it be Christians after our meaning; but of this I am sure, that in very truth they worship God. That valley is like Paradise for peace. The sight of it clouds the senses and makes the heart sore as a man's heart is sore for the home of his childhood. For us men of blood to enter the place would be great sin. I will have no part in violating so holy a shrine. We go to offer an alliance to the Grand Inca. But what need has he of an alliance when God's cherubim are on his side? If we fought and won, the gold and jewels would be our plunder. And the City would be the quarry of every ruffian from the four corners of earth. 'Twould be the offence against the Holy Ghost, and, sinful man though I be, I will have no hand in it."

The Admiral watched me curiously, and narrowed his eyes as if in thought.

"You say the priest gave you a drug to heal your wound. May it not be that the City you saw was a dream?"

"Nay, it could not be," said I. "There is no drug would set a man shivering on a rock with a storm behind him and the New Jerusalem at his feet."

"Then, Nathan, 'tis like the lost Atlantis," he said musingly. " 'Tis a City not of Time but of Eternity."

He opened his doublet and showed a jewel of gold which hung by a cord around his neck.[2] "That," said he, "is the badge of my quest for the Golden City. He who gave it me sought for it all his days, and, like you, saw it but from a hill-top. I cannot draw back from the search. But I think that when I go I will go alone."

After that we spoke no more of the business. I kept my own counsel, and the Admiral gave out to the others that I had found a certain way to Manoa, but had been held back from going further by shortness of time and his express commands. Amias Thyn, to be sure, told marvellous tales to his comrades, but he was so confused in his speech that he had no credence. Indeed the rumour spread that he had never ventured beyond the Indian town, but had lain there for a fortnight incontinently drunk...

---

1 Nathan Stubbs, captain of the ship *Good Venture,* told this tale to Master Samuel Purchas, who omitted it for obvious reasons from his famous *Pilgrimes.* Nathan's narrative, however, exists in MS, in a very difficult handwriting, and a copy is in the library of an Oxford college.

2 See Chapter 1

CHAPTER 5

Cadiz Bar [1]
(1596)

"Why, truly, your great enemy is the Spaniard. He is a natural enemy...by reason of the enmity that is in him against whatsoever is of God... And the Spaniard is not only our enemy accidentally, but he is providentially so; God having in his wisdom disposed it to be, when we made a break with the Spanish nation long ago."

Oliver Cromwell's speech to his Second Parliament,
September 17, 1659

...I have seen Sir Walter Raleigh but the two times in my life, and this was the way of them...

One May morning in the year 1596 I rode into the yard of the Bell Inn at the Shorne in Kent, and bade the potman bring me a tankard of small ale, for I had broken my fast early. 'Twas a chill morning, with flying showers of rain, and my horse was mired to the saddle girths. Presently there entered a seaman with a scarlet face, as if he had run fast and far, and on his heels a gentleman, all muddied with travel. The seaman shouted to the host to know if any mariners had been to the tavern that morn; and being told no, set off again at a run for the next alehouse. I could not but observe the gentleman, a tall man of noble carriage and a dress too rich for our country byways. He bade the seaman complete his tale of the taverns and return to him with a report, while he sate himself on a bench and, like me, called for ale. He had an air of weariness and perturbation, but his eyes were masterful and his mouth had a hint of humour. Indeed, as he sate himself on the bench and watched his lieutenant trotting out of the yard, he laughed outright.

"Your servant, sir," I said. "You are early abroad."

He looked at me very pleasantly. "My friend," said he, "I know not you name, but if you have any knowledge of the sea, you will grant that a man must rise early to outwit the absconding mariner."

"Why, for the matter of that," I answered, "I have had some small trouble of my own in the same quarter. I had much to do with the manning of certain ships against King Philip's Armada, and that was a business to whiten a man's hair."

He nodded approvingly. "Since you have served your Queen, you will have a fellow-feeling for the trials of a campaigner. Whew! I have the thirst of all the Guianas."

"You are with the fleet at Gravesend?" I asked.

"For my sins," said he, "I am by Her Majesty's command the Rear-Admiral of Her Majesty's Spanish Fleet."

I rose, doffed by hat, and bowed low. For I knew that I was in the presence of Sir Walter Raleigh. He nodded and smiled.

"I say 'for my sins,' for my rear-guard should have been at sea a week ago. Instead of which my ships rot in the Thames, and I spend my days hunting mariners through miry lanes. A thing to try hard a man's Christianity! But what do you here?" he asked.

I told my name and designation, adding that I had fought somewhat in Europe, and was but three months returned from campaigning in the Low Countries with Sir Frances Vere.

"You would rest at home," and his eyebrows ran upward, "while the Spaniard holds Calais?"

"Nay, sir," I cried. "I do but wait on my chance. I am ripe for another venture, but I am delayed and distracted by those who order affairs. I have offered my services a dozen times, but I am but a humble squire and can get no satisfaction."

He reached out a hand for mine.

"You shall fight with us, good sir. Never fear. And I have that to tell you which will set an edge on your valour… His God hath called for Sir Francis Drake."

The news took the breath from me. We were hourly waiting to hear that that grim sea-captain had sacked Panama and laid hands on all the Isthmus. I could only look with awe at Sir Walter's heavy countenance, and stammer "Where?" and "When?"

"A post reached me this morn from the Queen herself. He lies far off in Porto Bello beneath some great wave. 'Tis all over now with the English expedition. It must return leaderless, and we must strike at the Spaniard elsewhere. But mark you, there is no news on earth will so put heart into Rome and Spain. They feared Frankie as if he were the devil. Without him they will deem us no better than masterless men. 'Tis to disperse that dream that you and I go forth, Sir Adam."

I was so eager that I could scarce muster words. "You will take me with you, sir?" I said.

He wrinkled his brows in thought. "Nay, not with me. We are all seamen, and our task will be plain seacraft. You are soldier-bred, and your place is with the land force under my lord Essex. I will give you a letter to my lord, who will receive you gladly, for he loves me, and has an eye for a proper young man. The lord High Admiral is by this time at Plymouth, and with him my fellow in the rear-guard, Lord Thomas Howard. My lord Essex joins them there. And when I have writ a letter, 'tis for you to post thither without loss of an hour. With a fair wind they may sail any day, and suffer me to follow when I have gotten in my runaways."

The lieutenant entered, redder than before, but with a gleam of satisfaction in his fiery eye.

"I have laid hands on two, sir," he cried, "and the guard has 'em on the road to the water. There is tidings that five more of 'em lie drunk at Saxeleigh."

Sir Walter had written me a letter, using his own tablets, and ink from a horn fetched by the host of the tavern. He sealed it with his signet ring, and gave it into my hands.

"Now, Sir Adam, ride – ride for your life! We shall meet in a week or more."

"Where?" I asked, for I knew nought of the destination of the fleet.

"That is a secret," he said, laughing, "but I will give you a clue. We follow in the footsteps of Sir Francis Drake."

Then I knew that 'twas against Cadiz we sailed. I was confirmed by his crying after me, "Farewell, *Septimi, Gadis aditure mecum.*"

This was the way of my second meeting.

About noon of Sunday, the 20th of June, I was with my lord Essex in his ship the *Due Repulse* in the squadron of which my former General, Sir Francis Vere, was Vice-Admiral. A great dispute had arisen among the Admirals as to the attack upon the galleons in the inner harbour of Cadiz, the Lord High Admiral maintaining that 'twas needful first to silence the shore forts with a land attack, while my lord Essex held that, with a fine stern breeze blowing, 'twas our business to proceed forthwith against the ships. There was a great sea rolling in from the outer ocean, and we tossed uneasily at anchor while we endeavoured to land our footmen on a rocky beach where the surf broke heavily. Already the long-boat of Sir Francis Vere's *Rainbow* had been swamped, and fifteen stout fellows drowned. My lord Essex paced the deck, tugging at his beard, very fretful at the delay and the plan of which he little approved. Presently, as I stood near him, we saw in the hollow of the waves a cock-boat, rowed by two seamen, with a gentleman aboard her.

"What madman takes the water in that nutshell?" I asked, when my lord gave a cry of joy and ran to the bulwarks.

Then I saw that the madman was no less than Sir Walter Raleigh, the Vice-Admiral, who had gone to the inshore station the night before in his ship, the *Warspite*. He greeted my lord with a wave of his hat, and the next moment we had thrown him a rope, and he had clambered on deck as lightly as a squirrel, while the cock-boat was made fast below.

"What folly is to the fore, my lord?" he cried. "You are landing men on an iron coast, while God has sent us a fresh wind to bear down the galleons. They lie packed like pilchards in the inner harbour, hungering for shot. The four Apostles are there, and with two of them, the *Philip* and the *Andrew*, I have a score to settle for Dick Grenville's sake. Likewise, there is the Flota of the Indies, and the carracks of New Mexico. What tarry we for?"

My lord said moodily that 'twas the decision of the Lord High Admiral and the Council.

"Then I go to reverse the decision," said he, and moved to the bulwarks.

"Stop, Sir Walter," my lord cried. " 'Tis not fitting to discuss what the Council has agreed."

"Was it your will, my lord?" asked Sir Walter. "No. And judging by the wind He hath sent, 'tis no more the will of God. I go to talk with the Lord High Admiral."

My lord would have stayed him, but he was gone. He swung himself into the cock-boat, and the next minute was hid in the trough of the great green billows. My lord turned to me. "There goes a gallant folly. If he be not swamped, he will get the rough side of my lord Howard, and there will be but the more confusion. A pest upon a war where all are generals!" And he took again to his striding up the poop, but gave orders that for a little the landing should cease.

In about an hour there was a cry from the watchman in the bows, and we perceived the cock-boat returning. The tide was with it, and 'twas so engulfed in water that I looked every minute to see it founder.

" 'Tis good news," I cried. "See how Sir Walter waves his hand."

We lay over the edge while the boat neared, and there was no mistaking the air of the Admiral. He was steering, not for us, but for his own squadron, which lay further within the harbour. But he passed us at some fifty paces, and I could remark the exultation in his face. He was as soiled and draggled with the sea as any mortal I have ever seen.

He looked up at us, and, as he passed, cried but the one word in Spanish – "*Entramos.*" Upon which my lord Essex, transported with delight, cut a step on the deck, and, taking his plumed hat from his head, flung it into the sea in the direction of the inner harbour. "Glory to God!" he cried; "the tide will carry my hat to the galleons and give them my challenge."

By the time we had re-shipped the men from the shore 'twas close on evening, and, though my lord would have pressed on forthwith, like Francis Drake, in the darkness, the others were for waiting till daylight. Sir Walter came aboard to sup with my lord, and a council of war was held in the cabin of the *Rainbow*. I learned later that after much wrangling Sir Walter was appointed to lead the van with seven ships of battle – his own *Warspite*, my lord's *Rainbow*, the *Mary Rose*, the *Lion*, the *Swiftsure*, the *Dreadnought*, and the *Nonpareil*. As these were the lighter vessels, they were deemed fittest to come to grips with the galleons in the shallow water, while my lord Essex and the Lord Admiral commanded the greater ships of the main fleet.

We started at the first peep of day, Sir Walter having the lead of us. I remember very plain how merrily he sailed under the very walls of the City, while the forts battered him, and the galleys ranged alongside shot off all their pieces. He disdained to answer them, save that at each cannonade he had his trumpets sound a blare. But the others of our fleet were less scornful, and the galleys were driven to their oars so that they might escape into the straits of the inner harbour to find shelter among the great galleons.

Presently he was within reach of the *S. Philip*, and straightway dropped his anchor. The Lord Admiral had ordered him not to lie alongside, but to wait for fly-boats before he boarded. There was too little depth of water to deploy into line, and we had perforce to wait for the flood-tide, being anchored in the shape of a great wedge, of which Sir Walter's ship was the point. For three hours our English guns played mightily upon the Spaniards, and they in turn, being armed with the heavier artillery, replied with deadly hurt. The *Warspite* was shut from our view by clouds of smoke, and diademed with red jewels of fire. 'Twas the first time I had ever faced a sea-fight, and for a soldier 'twas a stern trial. Here was no breach to attack or enemy to regard; only the menace of countless great shot pouring like hail from an abyss of smoke and flame. We soldiers could but stand to our posts on deck, praying that the hour would come when with cold steel we might make return. Some of us were sore wounded. One of my lord's gentlemen had his arm shot off at the shoulder, and I saw a seaman laughing one second and the next a headless trunk. All the while the flood-tide was rising, and, being lightly anchored, we were drifting nearer to the galleons.

After an eternity of waiting, Sir Walter came to us in a skiff, his face so black with powder I had taken him for a negro. He implored my lord to send him the fly-boats, for without them he could not bring the fight to an issue.

"Fly-boats!" cried my lord. "I would give my left hand for the sight of them. There has been treason in this, Sir Walter, or else my lord Howard's wits have gone a-wandering."

"I wait no more!" said Sir Walter, getting aboard his skiff. "I can endure this battery no longer. If we wait we must burn, if we board we may sink, and either fate is destruction. They have the guns of us, man – two to our one, I go to shake hands with the *Philip*, and shall be aboard her before the Dons can cry 'Santiago!'"

Then began the most desperate strife I have ever witnessed. For between Sir Walter, my lord Essex, and my lord Thomas there was a noble rivalry as to who should first grapple with the galleons. Indeed, 'twas like a play of schoolboys; for my lord Thomas, pressing forward, would have drawn his ship alongside of the *Warspite,* but Sir Walter cut the warp. So it came that the *Warspite* and the *Swiftsure,* in which ship was my lord Essex and myself, formed the van of our English line at the mouth of the straits into which the galleons were crowded.

The flow of the tide set them straining on their anchor-ropes, so that they leaned over towards the shore. Their fire was slackening, for with the list of their hulls the great guns on their upper decks shot too high, and, though they cut our cordage and brought down our spars, they did little hurt to our crews or men-at-arms. I remember that Sir Walter flung a hawser, so that he might warp his ship along of the *S. Philip,* and fast as the rope was flung the Spaniards cast it loose, and heeded not our musket fire. There was a window of a poop cabin where grew a rose in a pot, a strange sight in such a mist of terror. With every motion of the galleon the little flower rocked, so that I found myself waiting on its fate, oblivious of what was a-doing around me. Such small things will hold a man's regard in a crisis, and to me that rose was the gauge of our toil. If it fell, I made sure that the Navy of Spain was conquered. A hand was stretched out at last and the flower drawn in; and at the same moment a bullet grazed my right ear, causing me to bleed like a stuck pig. Also I saw Sir Walter's hawser fixed at last, and the *Warspite* begin to draw up to the *Philip.*

'Twas the turn of the battle. The Spaniard had no heart for English steel. A trumpet blared, and the anchor-ropes of all four galleons were cut. They set in to the shore with the tide and wind, and the *Warspite* was like to have gone with them. But, seeing the peril, one of the seamen cut the warp with an axe, and she rode clear. Then ensued a horrid and amazing spectacle. All four galleons heeled over on the mudbank, and from ports and deck men were spewed like sea-coal from a basket. Many were dying of wounds, and there were dead men that rolled heavily like bales into the sea. The *S. Philip* and *S. Thomas* caught fire, and vented forth great belches of dark smoke, while ever and anon a keg of powder would explode and shoot red flames skyward. We on the *Swiftsure* were scorched with the heat, and choked with the fumes of it. Sharpshooters on the poop of the *S. Matthew* still kept up a deadly fire, while all the aim of our fleet was to capture the grounded galleons which were yet unburnt. There was no sign of fly-boats, and we could not with safety urge our vessels nearer the shore, so we must take to the pinnaces and long-boats and row through the reek to the mudbank where the *S. Andrew* and *S. Matthew* lay. The boats from the *Warspite* were there before us, and such a confusion began that if any had desired to see Hell, there 'twas most livelily enfigured. We set parties to pick up such of the Spaniards in the water as were yet alive, and would doubtless have saved more had not the boats from the Flemish ships come up and begun an accursed work of butchery. Indeed my lord Essex bade us fire upon that rabble, that they might learn the decencies of a soldier's trade.

Sir Walter was first aboard the *S. Andrew*, being eager to capture the galleon that had fought with Sir Richard Grenville's *Revenge*. But by this time all order in the fight had slackened, and those who had not swum to shore or been choked in the mud were huddled like limpets on the steep-sloping deck, clinging to cords and pins and whatever might give them hold. Yet one or two in the crosstrees still kept such havoc with Sir Walter's leg that he all but rolled into the sea. I chanced to be at his side, and gave him support, but 'twas a horrid wound, all interlaced with splinters of wood. Yet so great was his spirit that he had the strength to receive the submission of the Spanish Admiral before he swooned in my arms.

We had made prize of two galleons, and the others were but shells frizzling to the water's edge. I carried Sir Walter back to the *Warspite*, and had the wound dressed with such rough chirurgery as availed us. He was in a fury of impatience, for it seemed to him we were about to lose the fruits of victory. My lord Essex had ordered an assault upon the City of Cadiz; but, said Sir Walter, we have destroyed the City's defence, and 'tis like a ripe plum that can be plucked at will. A city cannot flee, but ships can, and beyond the Puntal Channel was the Indian Flota, laden with the tribute of the West. If we took it not now, he held it would escape us by the narrow channel to the south, so soon as the tide allowed, and be in some safe port by the tide allowed, and be in some safe port by the evening. He sent messengers to the Lord High Admiral and my lord Thomas and my lord Essex, but the mind of the Council was set on sacking the City. 'Tis a malady that burns strong in a man after a bloody fight, as I have witnessed in the Low Countries. They sent back civil words about his wound, and bade him consider his health and his value to Her Majesty.

Whereupon Sir Walter fumed himself into a fever. "There is naught for it, Sir Adam," he said, "but that you and I should go alone. I will take twenty-five men-at-arms and a score of sailors. The Flota will be but a lame duck now that it has lost its defenders. We will ship ourselves in pinnaces, and trust God to give us the wealth of New Spain. 'Tis the Guiana voyage repeated."

I implored him to respect his weakness, but he would take no denial. He gave the orders, and in an hour's time we were embarked in the boats, while from the shore came the first thunder of the great guns in my lord's assault on the City. That harbour was as strange a place as I have ever seen. Well might it have been called the Spaniards' Graveyard. For the dead floated everywhere, and the wreckage of ships, blackened with fire and reddened with men's blood. It was silent, too, for the captured galleons had been towed off, the lighter Spanish ships had fled inward, and there was no sound save the seagulls and a last spluttering of flames from the hulls of the *S. Philip* and *S. Thomas*. I remember that I wondered what had befallen the little rose-plant in the pot…

We were not opposed, save for some stray shots from the land, till we had gone through half the channel. Then beyond us we saw the tall masts of the Flota, and in front an array of galleys, the same which Sir Walter had saluted with his trumpets below the forts of the City. At the sight of them we let out a cheer, and our fellows bent fiercely to the sweeps.

" 'Tis the Plate Fleet," Sir Walter cried. "One more tussle, lads, and we have our hands on the treasury of Spain."

'Tis hard to stand against one who is newly victor, and 'tis doubly hard, if you be the keeper of treasure, to withstand a victor who burns for it. The sight of our grim faces sent half of the crews of the galleys overboard. There were some that kept their places, and we had two men slain in the first boat; but the galley crews were rebelling, and had out their sweeps even against the will of the soldiers, who would have fought. There was no need to board. Such galleys as did not flee before us were emptied of men, so that 'twas like sailing through a woodyard. "Twenty strokes, lads," Sir Walter cried, "and we are at the gold."

Then that happened which rebuffed our hopes, but did great honour to the Spanish nation. One instant we were looking at the Flota, with men on every deck; and the next the great ships seemed to fly asunder in a dazzle of light. The heavens were torn with the crash of it, and we of the boats crouched in the bottoms, expecting momentarily to be engulfed. Some timbers did indeed strike us, and there were men bruised and wounded; but, mercifully, we had not advanced near enough to suffer heavily either from the rubbish or the swirl of water over the sinking ships. The Spanish gunners had done their work well. When the air cleared, we sat moodily at our thwarts, rubbing our eyes and gazing into the sea which held the dust of a Navy. Far off we saw certain of the galleys fleeing to a south port.

Sir Walter's complexion changed from wrath to a sudden humour. He took off his hat and saluted the empty channel.

"Twelve million gold ducats," he said, "gone to the congers – and God knows how many human souls. They have learned Dick Grenville's lesson. I love not Spaniards in life, but some have a pretty notion how to die."

1 The story of Sir Adam Bontier, a gentleman adventurer with the fleet of Essex. Sir Adam, being taken prisoner later by the Spaniards at Cartagena, told the tale to a Dominican Friar, Jordanus, who left the record in monkish Latin in his monastery of Candelaria in Teneriffe. It was deciphered the other day by a Spanish geographer, and I have freely adapted it.

CHAPTER 6

New Times; New Men [1]
(1603)

"O what a noble mind is here o'erthrown!
  The courtier's, soldier's, scholar's eye, tongue, sword,
  The expectancy and rose of the fair state...
  The observed of all observers, quite, quite down!"

Hamlet III. i. 159-162

One bitter evening in the third week before Christmas, having finished my comments on the case *Doe against Thomas Altwhistle* for my master, Mr Serjeant Jodrell, I bethought myself of the need of supper. My lodgings above Middle Temple Lane were grown mortal chilly, and the single lamp by which I pursued my toil had turned so smoky and foul that 'twas worse than a farthing dip. My former servant was dead of the Plague, and I had to make shift with a wastrel out of Whitefriars, who mulcted me grossly and gave me small comfort. 'Twas the night for a tavern, and my thoughts dwelt lovingly on the roaring wood-fires and the excellent mulled ale of Gilpin's in Fetter Lane.

I went forth about six o'clock into a town which lay still as death under the stricture of a great frost. It had been such a winter as no living man remembered. A weeping summer had wakened the Plague, and in each week of September over two thousand died. Then had come an autumn of roaring gales, which purged the infection but slew the frail by scores. To this had followed a binding frost, so that ice crackled on the edge of the salt tides, and beer was frozen in jugs, and a man had much ado to keep the blood flowing in his veins. Also the land was disturbed by treason, and tales of Spanish invasions, and Scottish tumults. There had been the treason of the Bye, as it was called, for which the priests Watson and Clarke and my lord Grey of Wilton had been condemned, and the treason of the Main, for which my lord Cobham and Sir Walter Raleigh were to suffer death. For myself, I could make no meaning out of it all. There were some said that the aim was to bring the lady Arabella Stuart to the throne, and some the Infanta of Spain; but 'twas generally agreed that the Popish religion was to be set up and Protestant heads to tumble. At any rate, the priests had died a month ago, and this very day at Winchester the axe was to fall upon Sir Walter and the lords Grey and Cobham. I did not sorrow for their fate save that I had heard Raleigh highly reported of as a wit, and I had some regret that great parts and dishonesty should be so conjoined.

I found my seat by the fire at Gilpin's, and when I had turned the edge of my hunger took leisure to survey the company. There was a lawyer of Gray's Inn, whom I knew and liked little – a jackal of the King's attorney, Sir Edward Coke, who had learned the ill tongue of his master. There were several merchants of the City, notably Alderman Killigrew, whose voice was the loudest on earth, and Master Hilliard, a man reputed of vast wealth, whose ships plied between Limehouse and the Low Countries. There was a countryman or two, come up to Smithfield for the winter markets, and two men whom from their dress I judged to have travelled far. One was clearly a gentleman, though his face was browned like a shepherd's, and the other a great broad man with a fierce beard on his upper lip and the sharp blue eyes of the mariner.

The tavern of late had been filled with talk of treason and abuse of the traitors, and the Alderman was loud in the matter. The King had no more zealous friend than this haberdasher of Cheapside, and to listen to him you would have thought that he sat at the least on His Majesty's Council. He narrated the late lamentable plots, and was especially bitter against Sir Walter Raleigh. I questioned him, and he answered that the reason of his hate was twofold: this Raleigh's treatment of my lord Essex, and his harshness with unlicensed adventurers who had infringed the Virginian monopoly. It seemed that Master Killigrew had been laid by the heels under a warrant of Council for importing sassafras against the monopoly, and thereby lowering the market price. His wares were seized, and he was mulcted in a fine, and when he sought mercy from Sir Walter he was sent packing with little comfort. The thought made him choke with gall.

"Ay, sirs, he scorned me – me, the Master of the Worshipful Company of Brazenfaces, and by God's grace within seven years Lord Mayor of London. This scorner of God and true religion raised a sacrilegious foot against my quarters. I could not abide his choleric eye. But Heaven has granted me vengeance. I saw him on the 27th day of October being carried by Richmond in a coach with the King's officers. There was such a crowd that the horses could scarce win their way. I saw many of my worshipful friends, and honest prentice lads with their staves, and scores of hearty citizens come out to cry against treason. When he came, this Raleigh, this Court popinjay and silken deceiver, with his proud eyes and his hand ever on sword – Ods, masters, but it was a noble sight! You could scarce prevent the good folk from tearing him asunder. They shouted out their threats, and flung pipe-stems and stones and mud. 'Twas the vengeance of the people, seeing as they were but the instruments of the Almighty's wrath. I marked the mien of the crowd and there was no foolish tumult, but a grave resolution. 'Twas both mild and awful."

"Mud and offal," said Master Hilliard very clearly.

The Alderman swung round as he had been stung. But before he could speak, the broad sailorman got up, and, pulling his forelock politely, says, "Did I hear, sir, as how stones and pipe-sticks were flung at Sir Walter? I pray you for the names of those as done it, for Nathan Stubbs[2] would like to have some manner o' talk with them."

The Alderman looked darkly at the speaker, for he did not follow his West Country speech. On Master Hilliard he turned fiercely.

"You defend the traitor!" he cried, "against the righteous wrath of the people?"

"I defend a great man against a rabble," says Master Hilliard. "Sir Walter has broken my head ere now for my ventures when they ran counter to his own, but he would ever protect England and the merchants of England against the common foe. Why, 'twas this Raleigh that kept the narrow seas clear for us venturers and wrung gold out of a stone to pay for war-ships."

"He was a monopolist," said the Alderman, shaking his head like a sick dog. "And he loved war and display and the things that beggar trade."

Master Hilliard laughed loud as he filled the bowl of his pipe with tobacco. "Tell that to your Brazenfaces at their next sederunt. Why, man, but for this Raleigh you and your like would have the Dons' swords pricking your fat sides till you gave up your crowns and mumbled paternosters. Some day, when you hear the enemy's guns booming in the Thames, you will repent of your folly, and sigh for the man who kept your coasts."

"I liked him little," said Gilpin, the host, who was carving a sirloin. "He was no trencherman, and would not drink good liquor when he was in the way of it."

One of the countrymen took his mouth out of a pint pot. "Rawley!" he cried in his broad Leicestershire tongue. "He was a good friend to us graziers. I mind two years ago, when Her Majesty, God rest her, would have passed an Act to make every man plough a third of his land, this Rawley up in Parliament and spoke against it. 'I do not like,' he says – and I cherish his words – 'this constraining of men to use their ground at our wills; but rather that every man use his ground to that which it is most fit for, and therein use his own discretion.' God's truth, thinks I, for I will earn twenty crowns a year off pasturing beasts when I would lose ten if I ploughed the acres. Here's to Rawley's health, wherever he be!"

The seaman was still at the Alderman, pulling his lock and speaking courteously, "Touching that flinging of pipe-stems at Sir Walter," he was going on, when the gentleman who sat beside him pulled him down.

"Tush, Nathan, you will get no satisfaction out of that ox." Then, "Gentlemen all," he says, looking round the company, "Sir Walter Raleigh, who is now with God, was my very good friend. I have known him since we played together in boyhood, and I will uphold that the King has no loyaller servant or England a more valiant lover. I impugn not the justice of his sentence, but if he erred 'twas unwittingly, and this day he hath paid the extreme penalty. But one thing I affirm, and will maintain it with my sword: When the King's Attorney said he had a Spanish heart and plotted a Spanish invasion, the King's Attorney most foully and blackly lied. Sir Walter's soul ever loathed Spain as he loved England."

"Treason!" cried the shrill voice of the Gray's Inn lawyer, Cheape by name. "He speaks treason against the King's Attorney-General, and this hath been held no less than treason against the King's person. 'Twere misprision to listen calmly, the crime for which the traitor Raleigh hath this day died."

"Treason!" cried Alderman Killigrew in his bellman's voice.

"I know not the condition of the protestants," said the gentleman sweetly, "but if they be gently born I will make amends for my words. I am Sir John Buller,[3] a knight of Devon, and my sword is at their service."

Master Cheape was a man of peace, and he shrank back into his corner and blinked his eyes.

"Nay, no offence, sir," he says; "but I must uphold the honour of my great master and patron, Sir Edward Coke. He has riper wisdom in the law than any man living, and he deals not in idle words. He proved to the Court that Raleigh was guilty of treason on five counts and of misprision on three. I grant you that on certain points he had but the one witness, but that witness was my lord Cobham, who spoke against interest since he thereby lost his own head. Moreover, as I will show by the Act 1 and 2 Philip and Mary, 'tis laid down that in a case of treason one witness will suffice, and accordingly – ”

But he got no further. The door swung open, and there entered a tall man in long boots and riding cloak, whose face glowed like a fire from the bitten weather. He bowed to the company, and called for mulled wine and a hot pasty. There was that in his voice that bespoke the soldier, and his restless dark eye seemed inured to wars. 'Twas unfortunate for the Alderman that he chose that moment, when the newcomer had seated himself, to begin the discourse again.

“True law and good law, Master Cheape,” he said. “A man may sleep in his bed while the land hath Sir Edward Coke as a faithful watchdog against ravening wolves. It stands to reason that this Raleigh was a spy of Spain; for if Spain be an enemy of the King and his Council, therefore by plain logic he hath a Spanish heart.”

I was watching the new-comer, and saw his brows lower. He stretched a long arm and caught the Alderman by the neck.

“Recant those words, fat man,” he said, while his great hand swayed the head back and forward like a puppet-doll. “I have sworn to suffer no greasy citizen to defile that name.”

“Fetch the guard!” cried the choking Alderman.

“Ay, fetch the guard,” said the soldier; “I will fling them a piece of dead carrion when they come.”

'Twas so comic a sight that I could not keep from laughing; and since 'twas clear that the new-comer was doing no great harm, we did not stir to prevent him. The Alderman spluttered and gurgled, but, seeing no better way of it, he stammered a withdrawal and was released.

"What comes of English liberty," he cried, valiant as ever, when he had gotten to the far end of the room, "if a man cannot speak well of the law of the land without being throttled by a wandering bully?"

"I care not a fig for English liberty," the soldier smiled. "But I will let no gutter-blood spit venom on a fair name. The law hath its own defenders, but so long as Gervase Luttrell[4] lives he will defend the fame of the great Captain who this day hath declined on death."

At this Sir John Buller reached his hand to him, and we three in the corner by the fire fell to talking very pleasantly, while the Alderman sulked, the seaman smoked his pipe, the countrymen drank deep, and Master Hilliard baited Master Cheape. The landlord, fearful of another quarrel, and being of a merry disposition, called for a song, and having most dread of the soldier, pressed him for a catch.

"Nay, friend," says this Captain Luttrell, "I am in no singing mood. This day I have lost a friend and master, I ha' come post haste from Winchester, for I could not bear to see the axe fall on that noble head. I waited there after the trial, hoping to have speech with Sir Walter, but he was kept too close."

"You were at the trial, sir?" I asked.

The soldier nodded. "I stood in the crowd through all the days of it. You must know that I have served with Sir Walter, both long ago in the Irish Wars, and some six years since in the fighting in the Azores. At the taking of the town called Villa Dorta I marched alone with him in a rain of shot, while my knees gave under me, and he laughed lightly and whistled a song. But never have I seen such a height of courage in man as in that Court in Winchester. He stood there like a royal stag bayed by a pack of curs. There was a row of Judges and Commissioners, void and foolish men, with malice in their dazed eyes; and in the midst the Lord Chief Justice, who had been better employed in the pursuits of his youth, when he took purses on Shooter's Hill. Before them raved the King's Attorney with a brace of fat serjeants. 'Thou hast a Spanish heart,' they cried; 'thou art a Spider of Hell,' – 'twas their best argument. They had lungs of brass, and their mouths frothed with venom."

"Treason!"cried Master Cheape.

"Another word, ferret face," says the soldier, "and you will go through the window, bars and all."

"I never dreamed of such a sight," he went on. "I am unlearned in the law, but motherwit tells me that no man can be judged on the sole evidence of one who is a proved liar and recants what he says ere he hath said it. What more was my lord Cobham than a half-witted coward, who bleated whatever he thought might save his neck? The most that Sir Walter was shown to have done was to have listened too tolerantly when the man raved, and to have thought him more fool than rogue. But the King's Attorney bellowed, and the Lord Chief Justice nodded his foolish head, and told the Jury that 'twas high treason for a man to be offered Spanish gold, though he never received it and would die ere he touched it. And the Jury nodded in turn, and went to sleep. But when Sir Walter spoke 'twas like the north wind that clears a fog. He was courteous to all, even to the mongrels that baited him, but if ever reason triumphed 'twas on his lips. There were many in that Court who hated him before they saw and heard him, who left the place sworn believers in his greatness and innocence. Nay, there was a Scot to whom I spoke, who had been sent by the King to write a record of the trial. He said that when he first came he would have gone a hundred miles to see Raleigh hanged, but ere the close he would have walked a thousand to save his life."

I asked about the end.

"The Jury had been taught their piece, and spoke it correctly. They obeyed the orders of the Lord Chief Justice, who obeyed in turn the faction of my lord Cecil and the Howards. Sir Walter spoke nobly at the close, and asked only for an honourable mode of death. As for me, I was so blinded with tears that I could scarce see. I walked into the street, and when I heard a man speak aught against Raleigh I pounded his head on the cobbles. I' faith, I left some sore crowns in Winchester that day."

The street door swung open again, and an icy blast set the candles flickering. The man who entered was a lawyer of the Middle Temple, much of my own standing, one Master John Pym, out of Somerset. He came in briskly with a light in his eyes.

"Have you heard the news, Philip?" he cried to me. "The King hath reprieved Sir Walter Raleigh."

At that there was such a shouting as brought in the guard to discover the cause. The seaman Nathan Stubbs arose and, catching Master Hilliard by the waist, whirled him into a hornpipe. Sir John and Captain Luttrell called for wine, and pledged first His Majesty, and then Sir Walter, and last of all gave the toast of confusion to all traitors, naming no names. 'Twas easy to read their meaning, and the Alderman and the Gray's Inn fellow were black with wrath.

Then Captain Luttrell declared that he was in the mood for singing at last, and would obey Master Gilpin's behest. So in a great round voice he trolled these verses:

> The Almiranty of Santa Fee
> Guards to 'tend him had fifty-three:
> And pikes and muskets a goodly store,
> And long-nosed cannon, forty and more;
> And five great ships that tossed on the sea,
> Had the Almiranty of Santa Fee.
>
> Dickon of Devon had nought to his name
> But a ragged shirt and an empty fame,
> An old plumed hat and the Devil's own pride,
> And a worn old blade that swung at his side.
> But he hated Spaniards terribillee, –
> And the Almiranty of Santa Fee.
> The Almiranty of Santa Fee
> Had a laughing lady, fair and free;
> Gold in chest and wine in keg,

And pearls as big as a pigeon's egg;
And crosses and jewels so rare to see,
Had the Almiranty of Santa Fee.

Now Dickon came in with the wind, came he,
And burned the castle of Santa Fee,
Slew the guards and rifled the chests,
And tossed the guns to the sea-birds' nests;
And he said to the dame, "Will ye come with me,
Or bide in the ashes of Santa Fee?"

Then up and spoke the lady free,
"It's out of this prison I fain would be.
For I am of England, bred and born,
And I hold all yellow-faced Dons in scorn." –
"Oh, a widowed man this day I be!"
Quo' the Almiranty of Santa Fee.

Master Pym, though little older than myself, had a gravity beyond his years. He had a broad chest, and a head like a lion's, and the serenest blue eyes I have ever seen in a man. Long after, when he had come to great fame in the nation, I reminded him of the night at Gilpin's and of his joyful news. And he answered that Raleigh was the first of those who stood for the liberties of England, and that he and Sir John Elliot and the others of the Parliament but walked in his footsteps.

On this occasion he told his tale with dancing eyes. A post had come from Winchester to tell how, when his head was all but on the block, Sir Walter had been reprieved and sent prisoner to the Tower. At this very moment he was on his way under guard to London.

"The tide hath turned," said Master Pym. "The very mob which a month ago would have torn him from his keepers is now shouting his praises, and calling for vengeance upon them that traduced him. My lord Cobham will do wisely to keep out of their hands. Mark you, sirs, Sir Walter hath not always conducted himself discreetly. He hath been headstrong and over-proud, and hath confounded oftentimes his own glory and his land's welfare. But he hath stood manfully for England, and the great heart of him could not sink to the reptile ways of the common courtier. This trial hath purged his fame in all honest eyes. He hath shown such a spirit in the face of disaster that from his words will be born a new gospel for the people. In after days, when we have long been dust, no man will remember Sir Edward Coke or my Lord Chief Justice Popham save as those who, like Judas and Pilate, betrayed innocent blood."

"Blasphemy!" cried Master Cheape, who with a sad countenance was making ready to depart. " 'Tis an ill day for England when a jackanapes from the West will teach law to his masters, and confound black treason with innocence."

The other laughed pleasantly.

"I am no lawyer, Master Cheape, though I have studied law. But I will give you a word in friendly season. Make the most of the present, for the day comes when you will fare badly. Doubt not there is a new spirit coming to birth in this land. I will yet live to see its workings, and when that day comes 'twill go ill with lick-spittles, whether of Kings or King's Attorneys."

Master Pym said no more, for Nathan Stubbs was plucking at his elbow.

"A mercy, kind sir," whispered the sailorman. "You are a friend to Sir Walter, and I would have a word in your ear. You speak of his lying in the prison of the Tower. Tell me, is this Tower a strong place, or could it be taken by resolute men? There be twenty and more of us, lying at the 'Green Wife' in Wapping. We be all lusty fellows, and handy for a rescue…"

1 From the Memoirs of Philip Benedict, Esquire, of the Middle Temple; afterwards a Judge of His Majesty's Court of Common Pleas.

2 See Chapter 4

3 See Chapter 1

4 See Chapter 2

CHAPTER 7

Stone Walls [1]
(1612)

"Stone walls do not a prison make,
    Nor iron bars a cage;
Minds innocent and quiet take
    These for a heritage."

COLONEL RICHARD LOVELACE

In the spring of the year 1612 I was deputed by the Principal and Fellows of Brasenose College to journey to London on various matters concerning our lands, and likewise to bear the thanks of the University of Oxford to the noblemen, gentlemen, and scholars who had made gifts to Sir Thomas Bodley's new Library. Among these donors were my lord Pembroke and, what seemed to me a portent of generosity, Sir Walter Raleigh, who from his prison in the Tower, and out of the poor relics of his fortune, spared no less a sum than £50. My lodging was at the house in Holborn of my mother's cousin, Master John Hoskyns, the famed Serjeant-at-law, and one of the most admired scholars of the day.

We would walk together, discoursing of high matters, and visiting those sights of the City which were marvels to a country-bred man. On the afternoon of May-day, I remember, we took the air on the wharf by the river from which the eye looks to the terraced gardens of the Tower. There I saw a man pacing, his hands behind his back, and his shoulders bent as if in thought. Suddenly there came up a ship with the tide, her sails dropping as she rode to anchor. The man put his hands to his eyes and stared at the vessel, as if he had been a sailor on the look-out. There were other spectators near, and I heard a murmur in the throng that the prisoner was Sir Walter Raleigh. Judge how I gazed at one whose name those thirty years had flown through the mouths of men.

The Serjeant marked my interest. "This evening," he said, "we will go to visit Sir Walter. He welcomes his friends after supper, and you will find better talk in his chamber than in any tavern of the wits."

So it fell that the same evening I put on my best suit of laced velvet, for in London I love to dress rather as courtier than as scholar, and took a coach to the West Gate of the Tower. Master Hoskyns was a familiar figure, and we were conducted straightway to that part of the Castle known as the Bloody Tower, because of the deaths of King Edward V and his brother. We entered a pleasant chamber, with windows on two sides, looking on one hand to the Terrace and the river wharves, and on the other to the Lieutenant's bowling-green and pretty garden of roses. The place was handsomely provided, and a small fire of logs burned on the hearth. There I found company assembled – my lady Raleigh, who lodged near by, and Master John Talbot, and the famous Ben Jonson, who was declaiming a scene of a play. There were likewise a Guiana Indian, who waited as page upon my Lady, and a small lean-faced man with deep-set eyes, who I was told was His Majesty's Solicitor, Sir Francis Bacon. My Lady sat on a settle by the west window, busy with some broidery, while the others talked and listened to the poet, and smoked the tobacco herb in long pipes.

Sir Walter Raleigh was dressed richly in scarlet trunk hose and a blue velvet doublet, with a furred gown around his shoulders. He sat close to the hearth, for he had the ague in his bones, and suffered much from chilliness. I remember how kindly he bade me welcome, speaking to me of Oxford and the scholars of his acquaintance, but ever with a word to the others, so as to bind us all in one circle of discourse. He was already past the meridian of life, but till I looked close at him 'twas hard to credit it. For he bore himself gallantly, and his eyes had ever a spark of fire and a laughing humour. Yet his face was shrunken about the jaws, his brows were lined and seamed, and a web of crow's feet rimmed his eyes. In his hair and beard, though tended carefully, there were many threads of grey. 'Twas the face of one who, like Ulysses, had seen men and cities, and had dared whatever man may dare. There were moments when I thought of him as an elder whose day had passed, but at other times he had the free and radiant air of youth, so that he seemed rather a lion caged than an old man dedicate to the leisure of age.

We talked first of his great *History*, wherein Ben and Sir Francis Bacon were his allies. I have never seen such a devourer of books, or one who used his knowledge so aptly. He would puzzle Ben – no mean scholar – with a Greek line, and confound Sir Francis with a subtlety of Justinian's law. From the company of his books, he said, he drew more true comfort than ever from his courtly companions in their chiefest bravery. 'Twas honestly said, I doubt not, and yet it rang hollow. I could not look at those eyes and believe them wedded for all time to a lettered page.

Then at a question of the King's Solicitor the talk turned to matters of statecraft. Sir Walter had written a discourse on *The Prerogative of Parliaments,* and had had it copied for gifts to his friends. Holding this discourse in his hands, Sir Francis was for questioning certain of its tenets.

"There is but the one prerogative," said he, "which is a seamless robe and indivisible. If it be in His Majesty he cannot share it with his subjects, still less with any Parliament of subjects."

"True," said Sir Walter. "There is but the one prerogative, but as I read the laws of England, Sir Francis – and these last years I have read in them deeply – that prerogative is not in His Majesty's person but in his office, and that office is, as it were, a trust for the benefit of all. The law is the true sovereign. If his Majesty offend against the law fundamental, his deeds are void: and therein I agree with my old foe, Sir Edward Coke. 'Twas the lesson which the Barons of England read to King John at Runnymede."

"Then where is your royal prerogative?" cried the King's Solictor. "Sir Walter? Sir Walter! I fear you are treading dangerous paths."

Raleigh smiled, and with the tongs drew a coal for his pipe.

" 'Tis a simple matter, like all true ones. The King has his prerogative inasmuch as he is the guardian of the laws. If he err in his wardship, he forfeits the honours which belong to him because of that wardship. All the Estates of the realm are, in a manner of speaking, one body, and as the leg hath no claim against the arm, so Commons have no right against Lords or Lords against Commons, so be they perform their proper duties. But the brain and heart of the body I take to be the King, and 'tis his office to see that all others play their parts, and that the body, which is the realm, flourisheth by those rules of civil health, which I call the law fundamental of England. He dare not rule harshly, for in so doing he is harsh to himself. As I have written in my *History,* 'no cords have ever lasted long save those which have been twisted by love only.' If the brain bids the leg be still and move not, the leg will grow palsied, because it hath broken the law of the body, and in time the brain itself will die. 'Tis so with kingship."

"Then," said Sir Francis, "it would seem as if His Majesty had no powers save as watchdog over black-letter statutes. 'Twas a sore downfall for the Lord's Anointed."

Sir Walter's face grew grave. "There is no downfall, for the King is the State, and the law is the law of his own well-being. Be warned, Sir Francis. I honour kingship above all earthly honours, and I would see it flourish immortally. But if ever the King set himself outside the State and without the Law, his prerogative will turn to a thing of gossamer. Then you will hear the cry of the prerogative of the Commons, as in ancient Athens, and haply

Parliament will set itself as sovereign above the King – ay, and above the people."

The king's Solicitor flung up his hands and laughed. "A prison hath made you a prophet, but your vision outruns reason. I, who have some share in the governance of the State, have no such forebodings. I would strengthen His Majesty so that he become in very truth God's regent on earth."

Raleigh turned to me. "You will live the longest of us, for you are the youngest. Treasure my words, Master Bristowe, and when you are old consider if I have spoken falsely."

Ben had grown weary of the discussion, and was for singing a new song from a play called *Cymbeline,* but lately given to the town. 'Twas a dirge of the vanity of human hopes, about golden lads and girls who come to dust. He had got to the third verse when the door opened and a young man entered.

I had never seen him before, but the company knew him and stood up at his advent. He was a slim lad of some eighteen years, with a pale complexion, but ripe and masterful brown eyes. Sir Francis bowed low before him, and my Lady came forward with deep curtsey. But Raleigh took him by the hand and drew him to the fire. "Welcome, Harry," he said; "your ship is ready at last." And Sir Francis said, " 'Tis a chill evening, sire." Then I knew that the stranger was the Prince of Wales.

I know little of Courts, but the lad was as merry among us as if he had been Sir Walter's son. His coming dispelled all dull converse on statecraft and Ben's funereal ditties. Raleigh drew from a cupboard a little ship, the same in all parts as one which sails the sea. 'Twas fitted with mast and spars and cordage, and even little guns of brass. He set it in a slip on the table, and we clustered round to admire.

" 'Tis called by your name, Harry," said the maker. "As the *Prince* 'twill sail its mimic course, and I trust 'twill show the seamanship of its godsire. John Shelbury, and Keymis, and I have wrought hard at it for the past month, and to me the task has been like a cordial. The fingers make pleasant tools when the brain is rusty."

"As for cordials," said the Prince, "my mother bids me beg for a further supply of that of your own making. She hath three maids sick of fever... Pray, is that spar in the right proportion? Master Pett favours a heavier top-gear."

And so they talked like two shipwrights, while the rest of us waited, much tickled by this boyish play, for Sir Walter was as eager as the Prince. He had a tale for every item of tackle. This had been shot away at Cadiz in the *Warspite*, and that at the Azores in the *Good Venture*. And then fell to memories till the ship was forgotten. Candles were lit, and we sat round the May fire, while Sir Walter looked into the smoke-clouds of his pipe and told strange tales. 'Twas the highest pleasure I have ever got from the lips of a man. An hour ago he had been the statesman speaking of sober statecraft, but now he was Ulysses, telling of a new Phæacia and a better Alcinous. He spoke of Guiana and the great river whose shores gleam with gold, and the scented glades all hung with strange fruits which glow like lamps in the forest dusk. He told of harsh deeds on the Main, of fights lost and won, and of nameless heroes who took counsel from the lonely valour of their hearts. He spoke of Manoa, the City of Gold, which God hath hid in the innermost hills of Guiana, till the gates fly open before the chosen knight. And through all ran the tale of the Spaniard, who hath turned an Eden into a desert. 'Twas a voice from another age, for he spoke of Spain as the mortal foe of England, while that night in every tavern men were debating whether the Princess Elizabeth was to marry the Duke of Savoy's son.

I noted that the Prince sat with wide-open eye, the colour mounting in his cheek as the tales grew brisk. At the end he sighed.

"I have fear," he said, "that the Golden Age is gone from England, and we have declined upon the days of little men. The one eagle that hath remained to us we keep close in a cage like good poultry-keepers." He looked at Raleigh, who avoided his gaze.

When his gentleman came to attend him, he took farewell with the air of a boy still dreaming. He paused by the table where stood his ship.

"Ay, ay, good *Prince!*" he said. "You and I will never dip our flag to any cry of '*Santiago.*'"

When he had gone, Sir Francis Bacon shook his head solemnly, yet with mirth in his face. "How can the persuasion of His Majesty's Councillors anent the Spanish Marriage vie with a few old wives' tales and a toy ship?"

I visited Sir Walter again on an afternoon in July, when he received me on the Terrace outside his chambers. The Prince was with him, and their heads were close in their eager quest. Below the Terrace in the garden had stood a little hut of lath and plaster. The Lieutenant's lady had made it her hen-house, but now the fowls had flown, and Sir Walter had built a room of stout timber, where he experimented in the sciences. 'Twas like an alchemist's den, being heaped with strange simples and ores, and lined with alembics and crucibles and other vessels of the craft. By its side was a furnace where he assayed metals.

In the clear light of a summer day I could see writ on his face the ravages of time and the sickness of hope deferred. 'Twas nine years since first he had entered those walls, and every hour since he had struggled for liberty. The people had forgiven him his faults, if faults there were. To the commonalty he was one of the marvels of the City, a thing to point to their children and say: "There is the great Sir Raleigh." But his deeds had been done so long ago that only the elder folk clearly remembered them. To the world he was like Tithonus, a human shadow mated with the bright Dawn of a memory. At Court, as I had heard, his name was still a lively offence to the King and to those of his Councillors who favoured a Spanish alliance. 'Twas the very soul of irony that he should have been condemned for seeking the friendship of

Spain, and kept in durance because he was deemed Spain's chiefest enemy. But Her Majesty and the Prince of Wales were of a separate party and visited and comforted him, so that from this quarter his friends saw a sure hope of release.

Sir Walter was ever a lover of dainty clothes, and when he wrought in his still-room put on an over-garment, like the smock of a peasant. He had some copper ore from Ireland and a packet of marquesite from Guiana, and while they melted in the furnace he showed his store of herbs and spices.

"There," said he, "is the sweetest balm on earth. It grows in the high mountains of India, where no man can reach it; but the birds of the plains pluck it for their nests, and there the Indian seeks it. 'Tis Prester John's herb, and when distilled with cinnamon and crabs' claws is a sovereign cure for the falling sickness. I have but little left, for the ladies of the French King's Court have begged the most of it from me. A drop in a cup of wine will make a woman's eyes shine like the dew."

Prince Henry asked concerning the Great Cordial, which had made Raleigh's name famous above all physicians. Its maker held it cheap.

" 'Tis but a distillation of sugar and saffron, half made from an old wife's receipt in Devon and half from a device of the Indians of Hispaniola. Your quack will mumble charms over it and add noisome things to give it mystery, but 'tis only an old wives' posset for the common fevers."

Then the Prince, whose mind was ever on foreign voyages, fell to asking if Sir Walter in his travels had found no marvellous drugs among the people of the West. Raleigh shook his head.

"They have the bark of a tree which cures fevers, but I have long finished my stock of it. The Indian lives simply, and does not suffer from our surfeits and frenzies. But I have heard of a potion which gives a sick man strength and likewise the vision of the Blest."

We were eager to hear of this, and he told us how a Captain in his Guiana voyage had been shot by a poisoned arrow so that he lay at the door of death. A priest had healed him of his wound, and given him a drug which had strengthened him for travel. Then he had brought him to the top of a high mountain and had shown him a City of such golden beauty that the man's heart ever after was sick with longing.[2]

"That was a wondrous potion," he said, "but I am in two minds about the City. Sometimes I think that the virtue was in the drug, which, like the Turkish poppy, clouded his brain into a fair dream. Yet when I remember the stalwart rough fellow who drank it, I can almost believe that the draught did no more than comfort the body, and that he saw in very truth the magical City."

The Prince asked if the place were Manoa, of which he had read in Sir Walter's book in his Guiana voyage.

"It may be Manoa, of which there is good proof from the witness of other travellers, besides the belief of all Indians. Or it may be a better than Manao. Some day, if God wills, I may go and see." And he sighed.

Prince Henry spoke quick and soft. "I have news for you, Sir Walter. My father has promised me your release at Christmastide. He hath a plan for getting gold from the Indies, and he seeks your aid."

The words were but half heard by me, but I noted the sudden flush on Raleigh's face.

"If His Majesty fulfil the purpose of his great heart, he will find a devout servant. Nay, dear lad, we will travel together to the West in a new *Prince*, made on the model of your little ship. We will see together the great river Orinoko and the hills of El Dorado."

"And the forests and the toothed serpents and the pineapples," said the lad eagerly. "And we will talk with the Spaniard as Englishmen should. But 'tis an idle hope. I am tied by the heels, for my father says that it is not fitting that a Prince of Wales should go forth of the kingdom save in war."

"War comes," said Raleigh, "and all its battles will be fought in the West. You will yet hear your guns, Harry, a-battering Porto Bello, as Francis Drake sought. You will have your own topsails shepherding the great galleons to English seas. Fear not, lad. 'Twill be a merry world when England takes the water again."

We were now by the little furnace, watching the cup into which ran the molten metal. A thin bright trickle was crawling forth.

"Look!" cried Sir Walter sharply. "There comes the sinews of war. That is what all England will shout for – City and Court alike. Mark you, that is Guiana ore. I call it marquesite, to ward off thieves, but 'twas brought me secretly by Keymis from a mine I know of. 'Tis no marquesite, but pure gold, and there is the proof of it."

But the Prince had turned away. "Let us go back to the distillations," he said; "I am mortally wearied with all this talk of gold."

My last visit was made on a dismal day of November, when I had come to town with a petition to my lord Arundel on a matter of fines and recoveries. I found Sir Walter alone in his chamber, shivering by the hearth with a fit of fever. Outside the wind howled from the river, and the Terrace was a field of withered leaves. To my eye he had suddenly gone grey and old, and I saw that he was bowed with a great sorrow. Then I remembered the mortal illness of the Prince. All London waited hourly on the tidings of his death.

He gave me a wan greeting. "You find me in an ill hour, Master Richard," he said, "and my brain is too dull for converse. Sorrow rides the ass, says the proverb, prosperity the eagle. My wits go at an ass' pace these days, for I can endure my own ills, but my friends' woes make a woman of me."

I asked if he had news of the Prince.

"He enters the port of death. My own physician has seen him, and vouches that hope is over. 'Tis a malignant fever, of which no man knows the cause or cure. I sent him my choicest drugs, but they rallied him only for a moment. Had I seen the brave lad myself I might have read the riddle of his malady, but I am a prisoner convicted of high treason, and they would not bring me to him, though he cried for me."

Sir Walter flung his furred robe from him and walked to the window.

" 'Tis a fitting day for the passing of a king. Mark you, Harry would have made such a king as great Elizabeth was queen. He would have purged the foul humours of the land, and set England once more on the path of honour. I fear the realm hath sinned too deep, and his God will take him from the wrath to come."

I could say nothing but those Virgilian lines where the poet sorrows for the death of the young Marcellus. Raleigh spoke them after me.

"He was a son to me, and the solace of my captivity, and some day he would have been the greatest king in Christendom. He loved all honest things. He was a ripe wit and scholar, a wise statesman, and a dreamer of high dreams." He murmured to himself that verse of Theocritus which in English runs thus:

"But Daphnis went down the stream, and the whirl closed over the head of one most dear to the Muses and not hateful to the Nymphs."

Then, remembering that I was soon to be in priest's orders, I endeavoured to comfort him with the consolations of religion. He heard me with a sad courtesy.

"I bow to God's will, but submission will not chase away sorrow. I sorrow for myself, for I have now no good friend to bring me out of prison into the free air. But I sorrow most deeply for this realm of England. Nay, nay, Master Richard, I know what you would say. God will raise up another in His own good time, but for the present, as the Apostle saith, our case is not joyous but grievous."

Suddenly he flung open the casement. On the heavy autumn air came the sound of the tolling of a bell. 'Twas the Great Bell of

Paul's, which tolls only for a royal death. Then I knew that all was over.

Raleigh stood silent for a little, his lips moving as if in prayer. Then he turned to me, and I saw that his mouth was firm again and his countenance clear.

"I weep not for the dead," he said. "The Prince is now sailing brighter seas than ours. To our business, Master Richard! I am like to be many years in this place, and I must see to it that my time is well spent. Have you brought the digest of Suetonius I sought for my *History*?..."

1 A record left by that admiral scholar, Mr Richard Bristowe of Brasenose College, Oxford, afterwards Lord Bishop of Lincoln and Editor of the *Opera* of Seneca.

2 See Chapter 4

CHAPTER 8

Fairy Gold [1]
(1617-1618)

"The worn ship reels; but, still unfurled,
　　Our tattered ensign flouts the skies;
And doomed to watch a little world
　　Of petty men grown mean and wise,
The old sea laughs for joy to find
　　One purple folly left to her,
When glimmers down the riotous wind
　　The flag of the Adventurer."

The Ship of Fools

The Triangle Islands, off the Coast of Guiana:
December the Seventh, 1617.

This is the first hour of leisure since we sailed from Cork, and I take my Diurnal to set down the chances of the voyage. Two days after Sir Walter came out of the Tower, he bade me to go with him to the Abbey Church of Westminster, and was eager to know the names of all the new houses which had been built during his captivity. When we entered the Abbey doors he walked to the great new tomb of Queen Elizabeth, and stood a time in thought.

For long after he was sunk in melancholy, and spoke no word till he had come to my lodging in Chancery Lane.

" 'Tis the first venture," he said, "that I have made without the patent of my incomparable mistress. Times have changed in the land, and we sail on a desperate enterprise, with ill-wishers behind and an enemy forewarned before. I have written so much of late that I have much ado to rule the fleet. I pray you, Thomas, set out in writing all that befalls us, that it may be a record for those who come after me." So I take up my pen at my Admiral's command.

For near a year we were hard at work building ships and getting money. Sir Walter came out of his prison in March, and 'twas not till December that his new flagship, the *Destiny*, was launched from the slips of Master Phineas Pett. We had had trouble with our adventurers, scapegraces of honest houses whom their kinsfolk would have despatched with us to save from the gallows. Of gentlemen volunteers we had a better brand, for with us sailed Sir Warham St Leger, and Master George Raleigh, Sir Walter's nephew, and certain gentlemen of the Pembroke and Huntingdon families. There was trouble, too, over the Admiral's commission, and his pardon was misdoubted by his friends. There were those who said that the King wished no more than to get Sir Walter into fresh mischances, that he might use his life as bait for Spanish friendship. Spain's Ambassador, Don Diego, wrought day and night to frustrate our plans, and thought by offering a safe conduct for two ships to persuade us ancient sailors to put our heads in the lion's jaws. There were many said that Sir Walter only waited on the chance to turn pirate, and, once forth of the kingdom, would never show face again. But why set down the follies of his slanderers? All who had served under the great Captain knew the honour of his heart and his fearless bravery. Well we knew that he would return, though all Spain, and Hell, and every knave in England waited with open mouth to rend him. Knowing this, we had long thoughts of what might befall if the gold failed and the Spaniard met us with a superior force. But Sir Walter himself soon cast out these fears. In truth, he was drunk with freedom. His thoughts flew as happily to the sea and the West as a young maid's to her lover.

We were a motley company, for besides the adventurers I have spoke of, some of whom could not be denied from coming, we had among the crews many very perfect rascals, both French and English. In these days 'tis hard to get good mariners in England, for, owing to our lethargy on the sea, the stiff sailor-breed hath decayed, and those who once sought for El Dorado now seek only for pilchards. Nevertheless, some of our captains were true men, and there were some in the ships who had served aforetime with Sir Walter, and now dragged their legs from their firesides to share in his new venture. Knowing the nature of the crews, the Admiral published orders to discipline his thirteen ships and thousand men. He forbade all swearing, dicing, and card-playing, and promised to hang any man, gentle or simple, who should play the common pirate and conduct himself fowardly towards the Indians. To ensure that devoutness, without which great enterprises perish untimely, he had a reading of the Scriptures and prayers said night and morning.

We were royally feasted by Master Trelawny, Mayor of Plymouth, and the town drums beat our company aboard. Then came foul weather, and after being forced back twice to port, we anchored in Ireland in the Bay of Kinsale. Here of old Sir Walter had campaigned, and his friends flocked to greet him. My lord Boyle flung open to us his great house in Cork, and for six weeks we abode there, repairing the damage to our ships and victualling for the ocean. I will record a conversation with my lord Boyle, on a day when we went out from the town to fly hawks – a great sport of the Irish gentlemen. He examined me as to Sir Walter's standing with the law, and I told him my doubts. He whistled and pulled down his brows.

" 'Tis an ill trick," he said, "to set a gentleman playing with the dice loaded against him. It looks as if His Majesty were spinning a crown with Sir Walter, and crying for one face 'I win,' and for the other 'You lose.' If I were your Admiral, Captain Keymis, I would think twice before I ventured back to native land. Unless he get gold enough to make it worth the King's while to pardon him, he will be held scapegoat for every blunder in the last ten years. I hear he holds the King of France's commission. Let him take foreign service, as other honest men have done before him. I have risked money in the Guiana venture, but I would lose my share a thousand times ere I would see Sir Walter come to hurt."

I have treasured these words in my mind, but I have not yet found an occasion to tell the Admiral.

From Cork we sailed south to the Grand Canaries, and had sore trouble on the road with Cyrus Bayley, of the ship *Southampton*, who seized four French vessels, and would have plundered them. But the Admiral sternly forbade him, and bought from the Frenchmen what we needed for the price of sixty-one crowns. This Bayley was a violent, lying fellow, who deserted us at Lancerote, and went home to spread the report that the man who had restrained him from piracy was himself a pirate.

In November we came to the shore of Guiana and the mouth of the river Caliana. Affliction had pursued us over the ocean, and in the Admiral's flagship over forty-two men had died, including our best land-general, Captain Piggott; our only refiner of metals; and that renowned scholar Master John Talbot. Sir Walter himself was sick of a fever for a full month, and would doubtless have died but for the fruit we had shipped in the Canaries. 'Twas a voyage of strange portents. For five days we sailed through a hot tawny mist, and off the isle of Trinidad we witnessed a flight of fifteen rainbows, at which the crews were put in a mortal fear. The Admiral's sickness had set up mischief among the men, so that they wrangled without end and took ill to their duties. But now the portents we had seen brought a fit of piety, and they would attend the reading of prayers like choir-boys. I, who have all my life sailed the seas, rate our crews but lowly. They have not the spirit of those who sailed with us of old, neither as seamen nor as adventurers, being such as think more of pay than of extending the realm of England. The soldiers, two hundred and more, are of better stock, and our gentlemen are of good blood and high courage. God send we do not find a task too hard for our strength, for we have much rotten metal which will snap on the strain.

We lay in the bay of the Caliana for three weeks, till the health of our ship's companies mended. The younger men were eager to land, looking to see gold in every rock and an Indian or a Spanish captain behind every tree. The first to visit us was Sir Walter's Indian, whom he called Harry, and who had been with him some time in the Tower. He was a chief in the neighbourhood, and brought a great gift of new bread, venison, and all manner of fruits, which revived our wasted appetites. We hailed a Dutch vessel that passed by us, and by good fortune were thus enabled to send home those the sickest among us, including Captain Peter Alley, who since we left Kinsale has never moved his head from a deadly vertigo...

The expedition to the Mine has now been determined on. The Admiral is still so weak that he can scarce walk unaided; at any time the wind blows from the land his fever rages. Beside, there is the peril of the Spanish fleet, which we hear has been despatched from Cadiz: and the Captains are unwilling to venture up the Orinoko unless he remain to guard the river mouth. The Lieutenant-General, Sir Warham St Leger, is also sick of a dropsy, so it is resolved that both he and the Admiral shall wait behind with heavy vessels to keep watch in the rear of the expedition. It is further resolved to take the five ships of least draught, and embark in them a force of four hundred sailors and soldiers. These five ships are to be commanded by Captains Whitney, King, Smith, Wollaston, and Hall. Captain George Raleigh, the Admiral's nephew, leads the land force, and to myself is intrusted the search for the Mine...

I am burdened with the cares of my charge, and yet I am in good hope of a fortunate issue. When I landed first in Guiana there were no Spaniards on the riverbank. But now a new city hath been built, San Thome by name, which stands where the river Caroni enters the Orinoko. Of this project I heard when I journeyed thither in the year 1596, the year after Sir Walter's visit. But the Mine which had then been showed me by the Indians is thirty miles and more down stream, and but eight miles from the Orinoko bank, on a lesser river by name the Cumaca, and close against the mountain Iconuri. I have little fear of a Spanish attack, unless news sent from Madrid has caused them to guard all the waterways of the country. Sir Walter is earnest with me, for a good reason which I can well perceive, not to engage with the Spaniards save in the last extremity. He bade me camp between the Mine and San Thome, so that the soldiers could cover the vessels in the case of a sally from the town. He warned me expressly to risk no pitched battle with the Spaniards. "For, Thomas," he said, "a few gentlemen excepted, what a scum of men you have! And I would not, for all the world, receive a blow from the Spanish to the dishonour of our nation."…

Tomorrow at dawn we start, and Sir Walter hath given me his last commands. He bade me remember that his nephew, Captain George, was but a young man, and that he relied on my judgment. "You will find me," he said, "at Punto Gallo, dead or alive. And if you find not my ships there, you will find their ashes. For I will fire with the Galleons, if it come to extremity. But run I will never."…

The City of San Thome. January the Ninth, 1618.

I resume my Diurnal, but in dire despair and black sorrow. For the worst of all mischances has overtaken us. We have fought a bloody battle with the Spaniard. We cannot come near the Mine for the strength of our enemies. And young Walter Raleigh, the Admiral's son, is dead.

I have little heart for the tale of our ill-success. From the first I might have guessed that we were dedicated to misfortune, for all our five ships were foundered in the channels of the Orinoko, and 'twas three weeks ere we came together again and reached the plain country where the Indians dwell. The first news we had of the Spaniard was from an Indian of Assapana, who told us that a new Governor, one Diego de Acuña, had come post-haste from Spain. The name was that of the Spanish envoy in London, and I feared that it boded small good. Guns were fired on the banks several days at nightfall, but they did us no harm, and we believed them the work of forest Indians, who were ever ill-disposed. On New Year's eve, as I made my reckoning, we were near the mouth of the stream Cumaca, on which stood the Mine, and it was our purpose to sail all night, and in the morning of the New Year to land on the right bank of the Orinoko, some fifteen miles, as we thought, short of San Thome. But 'twas here we grievously erred. For, though 'twas unknown to me, the city had been transferred down the river to the mouth of Cumaca, and we sailed past its forts unwittingly in the darkness. Thereby we suffered the Spaniard to cut us off from the Admiral, and nothing remained but to fight.

We landed next morning and formed a camp, and that evening about nine we were ambuscaded by the Spanish and thrown into confusion. Nay, we had all been broken to pieces, had not some twenty of our gentlemen rallied and made a great stand. We drove the ambuscaders towards the town, of whose correct situation we were now but too well informed, and there by the walls we found the whole Spanish force drawn up to greet us. Young Walter Raleigh led the pikemen, and behind were the musketeers under Captain George. Now it is a rule of warfare that the men with guns should precede those with cold iron, that the shots may weaken the enemy before the pikes complete his destruction. But on this occasion all rules were forgotten, and we thought only of how quickest to drive the Spaniard out of the country. Around the town was a savannah, and in the moonlight we could see the steel headpieces of the Spanish gleaming above the high grass. Young Walter cried out at the sight. "Come on, my stout hearts!" he cried; "these be they who would bar England from the West."

Then I know not what happened, for I was with Captain George and the musketeers. I was told that the brave lad engaged the whole Spanish line, and fell with a dozen lance wounds in his breast. His last words were, "On, sweet lads! Lord ha' mercy on me, and prosper your enterprise!" When the pikemen saw him dead they were maddened to fury, and ere the musketeers joined them had overthrown the Spanish army. They slaughtered grimly and quietly, and Captain Cosmor with his own hand killed the Spanish Governor. Some fled into the town to the Monastery of Saint Francis, and these we slew, till by daylight there were no fighting men alive save such as had fled in boats to the river island of La Ceyva.

My first thought was joy, for I perceived that we had taken the chief Spanish fort in the countryside. But the next day, when I had taken counsel of Captain George, my mind changed to a great gloom. For there were we embroiled with Spain before we had proved the Mine, and if we failed in the latter enterprise we should be held no better than pirates. Above all, we had lost the Admiral's son, who was a most noble and gallant youth and the apple of his father's eye. My despair was increased when I found a parcel of papers in the Governor's house, and among them the plans of our voyage, which had been sent by King James to the King of Spain. Then I perceived very clearly that the words of my lord Boyle were true, and that, whatever befell, in England we should be accounted malefactors. What profit would be a basket or two of rich ore when we were a foredoomed sacrifice to ensure Spanish friendship?

We buried young Walter near the high altar in the church of San Thome, and in the same grave laid Captain Cosmor – him who had slain the Governor and had fallen later from a chance musket shot. Then I sat down and wrote a letter to the Admiral at Punto Gallo, setting forth my sad intelligence, and likewise forwarding to him the papers I had found in San Thome…

Meantime we are suffering much from sickness and famine. The Spaniards hold all the neighbourhood, and from the isle of La Ceyva they send out expeditions which cut off any Englishman who ventures abroad. The rabble of our men are ill-disposed, and but for the compulsion of the gentlemen among us would flee down the river or submit to the enemy. Would to God we had a hundred of the stout Devon lads who sailed with us twenty years past! Our single slender hope is the Mine, and I know not how to get to it....

January the Seventeenth.

Our case grows daily more desperate. Seven days ago I equipped two boats, and with Sir John Hampden and a matter a forty soldiers and miners, set out up the river Cumaca for the Mine of which I knew. Our men were in bad heart, for they saw a Spaniard behind every bush, and were weak with the heat and the low feeding and the rotten water. When I had travelled this way before, it had been through friendly country where no ambuscade was feared, therefore I had not marked the land with the care which a soldier gives to a hostile territory. I purposed to keep to the river till the Mine was reached, and then fortify a camp to dig for ore. By starting in the dusk of early morning I thought that we should escape the notice of the Spanish on the isle of La Ceyva.

But some traitor had told our plans, and ere we reached the isle their boats ran out from the shore and opened a brisk fire so that nine of those in the first of our boats were wounded or slain outright. At this they fell into a panic, and cried to be led back; and as we had no guess at the number of the foe, myself and Sir John resolved to return to the town for a larger force. But when we with difficulty reached San Thome, Captain George Raleigh was urgent with us to let the project sleep. I laboured to make him understand that in the Mine lay our sole chance of salvation. He replied that, having fallen out with Spain, there was no hope of mining, but the most we could do was to push on up the Orinoko to get Indian allies.

He left me yesterday, taking all the boats and a hundred men. So low have we fallen from death and the taking of prisoners, that I have scarce a hundred remaining to hold the town. I dare not leave the walls, for we are hourly attacked, and since many of our fellows are light-headed from sickness and stray beyond the defences we lose men at every assault. God help the poor souls who fall into Spanish hands, for they will suffer the torture which I have seen long ago on the Main! I have warned them of these terrors, but the most be such scum that they cannot of their own will choose a manly death…

February the Tenth.

Yesterday Captain George returned down the river, with no news save that ten of his men were dead of fever. It seems that the chief, Topiawari, who loved Sir Walter, is long dead, and the people so reduced by war that they can show no force against the Spaniard. We in the town have suffered in the meantime more than flesh can bear. No man dared sleep, for at all hours our enemies beset us. They made a cross in the sight of the walls and crucified thereon two of our sailors, so that we were beside ourselves with panic and sick with fury. We could not attack them, for they were everywhere in the savannah, lurking among trees and holes; but our weak defence was but too easy a target for their enterprise. By God's grace we have held the city, but I have now scarce ninety men, and these the weakest and most knavish of the crews…

We have held a council, and are of a mind to return. Captain George says he cannot hold his men, and Lord knows my fellows would break at the first chance. I am tormented by thoughts of the Mine, for from my window I can see the Mount Iconuri as near as Richmond Hill to Wapping. I need but a basketful of ore to give a colour to our honesty; but 'tis as remote as if 'twere Manoa itself. We are resolved to fire the town, and, carrying what spoil we have got, to hasten down the river to the ships at Punto Gallo. Even now we are piling grass and preparing torches. I know not how to face my Admiral, whom I fear I have foully betrayed. Yet I have done my utmost, though the issue is vanity. Would to

God I had laid my bones by young Walter, for I foresee no peace for me on earth…

Off Punto Gallo in the Isle of Trinidad. March the Third.

I am an old voyager, but I think my ventures are over. Yesterday at nightfall we reached the Admiral's ship, and found Sir Walter so aged by fever and sorrow for his son that I had scarcely known him. There were black looks and bitter words as I went on board the *Destiny*, for the tale of my failure had spread, and all men blamed me as the author of the expedition and its chief destroyer. Little I cared so long as I had the heart of my master. But Sir Walter received me with strange glances and a face of death.

"Where is the gold," he says, "with the promise of which I have bought my life? Where is the gold you boasted of, Thomas?"

I stammered my tale, but he scarce listened.

" 'Twas fairy gold," he said, with dreamy eyes. "We have both been to the rainbow's end, I fear. But I trusted in you, Thomas, and now there is no salvation. Cerberus with a hundred heads waits me, and I have nothing to stop his mouth."

All this he said so gently that it broke my heart. I fell to weeping, and dropped on my knees by his feet. When I looked up his face had turned to wrath.

"You let my son be slain," he said. "After that, what mattered it how many fell? Though it had cost you a hundred men to take the Mine, 'twas your plain business. Make me no excuses, Captain Keymis. You have failed miserable in your duty, and must now answer to His Majesty and the Council. God wots I have enough on my shoulders without taking the burden of your cowardice…"

I came back to my cabin with a dizzy head. I prayed that this anger would last, for 'twas less terrible than his sorrow. All evening I sat writing a letter to my lord Arundel, setting forth my case, for he was a chief promoter of the Expedition. Food I have not eaten for three days, but I thirst exceedingly…

This morning I have taken the letter to the Admiral to seek his approval. But he would have none of it. "I pardon all things," he said, "to him who serves faithfully; but you have betrayed me. You must bear the burden of your treason alone, for I will have no share of it." Then he turned away, and when I asked if this were his fixed resolution, he said he should have no other.

Then my mind filled with a great clearness. I saw that I had erred, and that in a desperate venture I had been too little desperate. I thanked God for his anger, which was merciful and right, for had he been kind and sorrowful I should have been tortured beyond human bearing. I told him that I saw my folly, and knew what course to take. "I have sinned," I said, "and welcome my punishment. But I claim a boon for old fellowship's sake. Grant me your forgiveness, that I sleep easy."

"I forgive you," he said in a weary voice. "I cannot cherish resentment, for I have no heart left in me."

I am lodged in my former cabin in the *Destiny*. Above my couch there hangs a picture of the Magdalen which Sir Walter gave me, for he loved to take pictures with him on his voyages. Even as Christ was merciful to that sinner, so I pray now His mercy on me.

There is no other way of it. I must run to port. If I die all men will blame me, and haply some of the load will shift from Sir Walter's shoulders; whereas if I live and return to England, I will but confuse matters; for I have a foolish tongue and small discretion, as was seen long ago in Lord Cobham's business. I am an old hulk, now these fifty years at sea, and 'tis time I found a haven.

I write these words more especially for the eye of Sir Walter, who will find them at my death. I have followed him through good and evil fortune; and now, to my grief, am the innocent cause of his undoing. God made me a frail man, full of fancies and prone to foolish confidence. But I have ever been loyal in heart to the greatest Captain I ever served, and I ask no boon of God but that He deliver him from his distresses, and forgive the manner of my death, seeing that my purpose is honest. I have no kith nor kin. For my fame I care not, but I would pray Sir Walter to think of me as I was in the days when we first adventured to Guiana. I say no more. Last year's nest is empty, as the Spaniards say...

Lest any man be suspect, I write that I die by my own hand – by pistol, if the powder be not damp, or by my Turk's dagger. The pistol Sir Walter gave to me long ago...

1 From the Diurnal of Captain Thomas Keymis, of the ship *Centaur*, preserved among the papers of the Fynes family.

CHAPTER 9

The King's Path [1]
(1618)

"Go, Soul, the body's guest,
    Upon a thankless errand:
Fear not to touch the best;
    The truth shall be thy warrant:
Go, since I needs must die,
And give the world the lie.

Tell men of high condition,
    That manage the estate,
Their purpose is ambition,
    Their practice only hate:
And if they once reply,
Then give them all the lie.

Tell fortune of her blindness;
    Tell nature of decay;
Tell friendship of unkindness;
    Tell justice of delay:
And if they will reply,
Then give them all the lie."

SIR WALTER RALEIGH

...I have never seen such a crew of pitiful mean rascals. The most had the visages of dockyard rats, and souls as ill-favoured as their skins. They had come out for lust of gold, and thought only that their pockets were empty, though God knows 'twas their own cowardly and rebellious spirits that made them so. I mind when we lay at Punto Gallo there was a pageboy spread a tale that Sir Walter's cabin was full of money. Presently some of my fine gallows-birds conspired to set the Admiral ashore and sail off with his flagship and his treasure; and, being of so weak a spirit, came crawling to me to seek my leadership. I drew my sword, and with the flat of it gave them a mightly lesson, and then with the point of it drove them forthwith to the Admiral, and discovered to him their treason. Figure to yourself the situation of a gentleman in such knavish company!

You must know that, with Captain Keymis dead and half our force destroyed, we had given up hope of success in Guiana, though the Admiral was still hot for a return to San Thome, whence he promised to bring a load of gold or leave his body by his son's. His captains looked coldly at the project, and some of the baser sort were all for remaining in the islands, and overhauling Spanish ships from the Main. Piracy is but a dirty trade, but I held this to be no piracy but lawful war, seeing that Spain has ever treated all English voyagers as trespassers worthy of a felon's death. 'Tis idle, I held, to prate of peace when there is no peace, and in the Indian Seas there is never aught but war. Had I followed my own will I would have favoured this enterprise, but Sir Walter was set against it, and I had no mind to cross his purpose. So I opposed the designs of the captains, and warned the Admiral that mutiny was in the air. But the boldest commander on earth cannot hold a flotilla of rebels, and at the isle of Granada the captains Whitney and Wollaston sailed away on their own errands. I have heard no more of them. I trust their traitorous bodies have long ago decked a gibbet at Cartagena.

We purposed at first to make Sir Walter's colony of Virginia, to victual our ships and rest our men, with the notion of seeking

Guiana again next year. But the temper of the crews was such that, had we landed at Virginia, they would have fled to the woods or joined the corsarios that frequent these coasts. Presently Sir Walter, whose mind moved slow from his great sorrow, came round to another opinion, and at a council of war – which I attended as chief of the soldiers during Captain George Raleigh's illness – it was resolved to sail for home. We stayed awhile at St Christopher's Island, while the Admiral wrote letters to the King. These he sent home in his fly-boat by means of his cousin, Master Herbert, and with him he despatched the idlest and most rebellious of the crews. Had I been Master Herbert I would have feared for my throat in the company of such a rabble. But it seems that God favoured gallantry, for I have heard that he reached England in safety.

You must know that we hourly expected news of the Spanish galleons, which had been sent out to take us captive. Our captains were in great terror of falling into their hands, for they had some knowledge of the tender mercies of Spain, and we had no more than four ships. Had we sailed the straight course for home, it was feared we should meet with this fleet or other Spanish ships of war, and we were in no mettle for fighting. Sir Walter advised that we make our course due north by the isle called New Found Land, from which there is a way to England over a narrower ocean. When we sailed from St Christopher's our fleet was the Admiral's *Destiny,* on which I sailed with the best part of the fighting men, while Sir John Ferme, Captain Pennington, and Captain King had the other ships to charge. I thought ill of these captains, save only King, who was an old lieutenant of Sir Walter's and a stubborn, honest, rough fellow.

We saw little of our consorts, for off the coasts of Virginia we came into a nest of storms, and were sore delayed for more than a fortnight. By the first days of May we were well into the northern seas, where the winds cut like sword-blades and the mist would wrap us round in chilly garments. Those who had sailed this way before were in mortal fear of floating ice, which comes down from the Pole, and has wrecked ere this many a goodly ship. Half of us were ill of the scurvy, and, though the sharp air had cured us of the common fever, we were taken with fits of ague and rheum so that scarce one man was free of sickness. In my day I have seen many companies of broken men, but never have I beheld a crew so desponding and weary as sailed with us those wintry waters. Ill-fortune takes the steel from a man's heart, and that rabble of ours were but yeast and mire. First they moped and despaired, and then they threatened, so that soon every man had a dark countenance and murder in his eyes. Meantime in his own cabin the Admiral sat alone with his grievous thoughts.

One day I sought him and bade him be wary. "There are those here," I said, "who bear you little love. You may find a knife in your back some fine morning."

" 'Twould be welcome," he said wearily. "Do you think I have any room left for fear, when I have buried my all? As well a shipman's knife as any other ending."

"Nevertheless you are our Captain," said I, "and if you fall 'twill go hard with my honest self and a score of lads who trust their lives to me."

"Then take the lead," he answered. "I am no better than a passenger. Sail where you please, my good Jacques, so long as you leave me alone." And he turned wearily away.

The Admiral had long cast a spell over me, so that I loved and reverenced him. But now God's hand was heavy upon him, and I was fain to ease his burden. With his consent, I took upon myself the captaincy, and I promise you I brought that rabble into some order. There were twenty lads who had fought by my side in the Low Countries, and with their aid I kept a fair discipline. I could see anger and scowling wherever I went, till soon I fancied that a seaman's knife was more likely to find my back than Sir Walter's.

One night as I sat alone at supper – for Captain George was still sick, and Sir Walter supped alone – a page-boy came down the ladder as though the Devil were at his heels. He bumped heavily on the floor, and when I picked him up showed a face like a dish-clout.

"Mutiny!" he cries. "They are cutting throats in the fo'c's'le. The men have got at the muskets, and are fighting for the powder-barrels."

It took me no longer than a breath to spring up the ladder and run down the deck to the forepart of the ship. We were rolling heavily, and I near broke my head on the bulwarks. I heard no shot, but from the fo'c's'le came the murmur of men in close and deadly conflict. I had rather hear a yelling like wild cats than that desperate hum.

A fellow had been set with a musket to guard to fo'c's'le ladder. There was but the one thing to do. I jumped clean down the steps, alighting plump on his shoulders, and knocking man and musket endways. In a second I was on my feet,

Roaring to the dogs to lay down their arms. I saw what I had feared. Some half-dozen of my lads were pinned in a corner where a door led to the powder store, and against them was a great press of seamen fighting desperately with dirks to win an entrance.

My shouts won a moment's respite. A dozen faces turned on me, their eyes bright with panic and murder. Then I reflected that I had no sort of arms.

"Every dog to his place!" I roared. "I have a gunner now standing by the powder. In three minutes, if I forbid him not, he will blow this ship and all in it to the skies. I care little for death, but the sight of you will cheer the Devil."

They believed me, or at any rate the resolution in my voice awed them. The press slackened, and I tore men out of it till my fellows could breathe. Help was on the way, for I was the ladder-hole filling with my men-at-arms. I was half stifled, but by dint of much buffeting I got the mob separated, and presently had the muskets and knives from their hands.

The worst I had pinioned and set soldiers to guard them.

"Now," said I, "I am about to hold an inquisition. You will assemble on deck, and I will have the truth of this conduct."

I had them drawn up by the foremast, the leaders in my soldiers' charge, and the others, a sullen crowd, huddled against the bulwarks. A pale moon shone from a watery sky, and ever and anon a wrack of cloud would darken the heavens. A lantern swung from a nail on the mast, flickering with every gust. I sat down on a barrel with a pistol on my knees. "Now for the meaning of this treason," said I.

At first no man spoke. Then, when I promised hanging, a fellow found his voice. He had an honest, foolish face, and I had marvelled to find him in the business.

"We fear to go back," he said gruffly. "Some of us have fallen out with the law, and if we land in England will march straight to the gallows."

"Ay, I can well believe it," I said. "And to your former ill deeds you have added mutiny on the high seas, for which hanging is too easy a shrift."

The fellow was still resolute. "We came out to Guiana in hope of gold, so we look to save our necks. It is but human nature, master."

"How many of you be gallows-birds?" I asked.

It seemed there was a round dozen, and their crimes were pitifully small. One had stolen beyond the value of forty shillings. Another had lain in Exeter jail for cattle-lifting, and had broken prison the night before his hanging. One had fired the stacks of an enemy; one had slain an innkeeper in a brawl; while still another had beaten a King's Justice for old scores. My heart warmed to such trivial malefactors.

"If that be your grievance, lads," I said, "I can promise that it will be mended. The Admiral will land you in Ireland, that you may be out of the King's danger. I have no love for the laws that oppress the poor and let the rich go free. Keep your minds easy. But, touching this late conduct of yours, you will go on bread and water for five days. And those who incited it will have twenty lashes apiece. To your quarters!"

But no man moved, and I could see by their eyes 'twas no common mutiny. The same fellow spake again: "Your pardon, sir, but we have not showed all that is in our hearts. We would save our own necks, but there is another neck in deadly peril. Whatever our danger from the law, the Admiral's is tenfold greater; at least so folks say. He is going home to death. We would restrain him, master."

Then I cursed them roundly, for venturing to lay their idle tongues to Sir Walter's name. I banned them up and down the skies for presuming to interfere with their betters. But the same thought had always been in my own head, and I was amazed to find so much reason in the swabs.

The man never winced, but looked at me with honest, dog-like eyes.

"Presumption or no, master, it is death for Sir Walter, and we of this ship would save him. We know him for a good captain, and would plead with him and keep him out of England. He hath many crows to pluck with the Dons, and here is the whole ocean for the plucking. We think as how he can serve England better by keeping the high seas than by putting his neck under the King's girdle."

I told them I had heard enough, and sent them packing. But the fear of those tarry-souled knaves had infected my own thoughts. I went to Sir Walter's cabin, but found him asleep. As I knew that of late he had slept little, I had not the heart to wake him, but retired to my own quarters and meditated till the small hours.

Next morning we were come into a pleasant sea, with the sun shining and a favouring west wind. I went to the Admiral and found him on deck sniffing the breeze – the first time for days that he had been forth of his cabin. He faced me with a brisker countenance and gave me a cheerful good-morning.

"Last night I slept," he said. "For little I contrived to forget, and this morning I am the better for it. You look grey about the eyelids, Master Jacques."

"I have cause," said I. "Last night, while you slept, I was quelling a mutiny… Nay, nay, sir, do not mistake. I have no hurts. 'Twas an innocent and weakly rising. We carry some gallows-birds aboard, and they feared to land in England. In your name I promised them the boon of Irish soil. But they pled for more than themselves, for there is a kind of decency in the rascals. They are mortally concerned about their Admiral's fate."

Raleigh looked far out to sea. "There is a magnanimity about salt water," he said. "It tinctures very sorry knaves with kindliness. And what would they have me do?"

"Like them, evade England. I think they would have you turn pirate, that you may get back from the galleons something of what Spain has cost you."

"And your thoughts, good Jacques?" he asked.

"Oh, as for me, I think piracy a sorry trade, but under your flag 'twould be fair and equal war. I have pondered the matter during the night watches, and this is my counsel. You are too great a leader to waste on the scurvy tribe of your ill-wishers. You hold the commission of my good master, the King of France. I will steer you to a French port, where you will be nobly welcome. A way will be found to repay all who have embarked their substance in this venture. Then, sir, you and I will take the sea in a King's ship, and with us will go the best blood of France and England. 'Fore God, we will harry Spain till no galleon dare put its nose outside Cadiz Bay."

"And this is your considered counsel, Master Jacques?" he asked.

"My considered counsel, sir," I said.

He walked a few paces up the deck, his chin on his breast. Then laid an arm about my shoulder.

" 'Tis not mine," he said. "You tempt me, good friend, but more by your loyalty than your designs. 'Twould be a heartsome task to sail the seas with you and twenty honest gentlemen. I am not so old but my blood stirs at the thought. We should make a gallant company, Master Jacques – you and nephew George, and

Jack Carew, and a dozen of your Breton sea-dogs. We should harry the Dons and be outlawed by every Court in Europe. Nay, we might restore that old warfare between Spain and England, without which there can be no lasting peace. But 'tis a boy's dream. For, mark you, I have left something very precious behind me in England which I must ransom."

I looked my bewilderment.

"My good fame," he said. "I have ever faced my destiny. You would not have me run from it at last. Look you, I have stood before all England for something which is half forgotten. I have preached the Gospel of an Ocean empire and of plantations in the West. I have urged that if England is to stand high in Europe she must fight her battles overseas. Of late few have heeded me. I was like an owl hooting in the churchyard among things dead and moss-grown. But this expedition hath wrought a change. The eyes of England are again upon me. Had I won, the King and his Council would have swung round with the new tide. But I have failed, you say. Ay, but there is hope for my gospel, if none for me."

I began to see light in his argument.

"What would become of it," he asked, "if I fled the land? 'Raleigh,' all would say, 'is turned pirate and Frenchman.' They would not blame me, but to England I would be as dead. I would have shrunk from my last duty, and God does not prosper a coward."

"But, sir," I said, "if they slay you, what becomes of your high plans?"

He smiled in his odd, subtle way, his eyes looking far into some untravelled country.

"They will flourish, for my blood will water them. *Sanguis martyrum semen imperii*. These last days I have been reading in Plutarch of Julius Cæsar, and find much comfort. For mark what Julius did. He built the Empire of Rome, but the Empire would not have endured but for his death. 'Twas Brutus' dagger that sealed the work. I have often a fancy that the great Julius knew of the plot and welcomed it, for he believed that such a structure must be baptized with the blood of the builder."

"You choose death, then, of your free will?" said I. "I am an old campaigner and have often faced it, but God knows I have not the heart to walk to it with so calm an eye."

He smiled sadly. "Your flattery is ill-placed. I have nothing to live for but my dreams. I have buried my dear son, and for my wife I can best save the poor relics of my fortunes by returning home. My old companions are all dead and forgotten. I have only dreams to furnish my bare house of life, and for those dreams I must spend what remains to me."

I could have wept at his words, but 'twas not for me to frustrate so high a nobility.

"Will you tell the crews?" I asked hoarsely. "They are in an ill temper, and will heed only you."

A trumpet blew the assembly, and yesternight's mutineers, besides my loyal fighting-men, gathered below the poop. Raleigh stood by the rudder, looking cheerfully as if he had a pleasant tale to tell.

"Dear hearts," he said, "it has been told me that you are concerned about the future. Fear not, for I will land no man in England against his will. Those who desire it I will put ashore in Ireland with some provision for their sustenance. It has been told me also that you grieve for the fate of your Admiral, and would have me keep the seas or seek a French port. Your charity stirs me greatly, but you waste your pity. I have nothing left to me but my honour, and I go to redeem it. Think me not boastful, but I hold death as no more than a thistle's down, if thereby I can come to my desire. If they slay me, England will think the better of me, and in a hundred years men's minds will turn to my thoughts, and see their worthiness. Fear not for me, brave lads. 'Tis for England's sake and her unborn people's that I must return. You would not hinder me from so great a joy?"

There was no answer from the crews, but there were few dry eyes among them. And these were the fellows who twelve hours before would have flung us both into the sea!...

1 From the notes of the Frenchman, Jacques Pommerol, who afterwards forsook the sea, settled at Louvaine, and wrote an epic in the classic manner on his adventures, which he called the *Jacquesiade*.

CHAPTER 10

The Last Venture [1]
(1618)

"Give me my scallop-shell of quiet,
    My staff of faith to rest upon,
My scrip of joy, immortal diet,
    My bottle of salvation,
My gown of glory, hope's true gage;
And thus I'll take my pilgrimage.

Blood must be my body's balmer;
    No other balm will there be given;
Whilst my soul like quiet palmer,
    Travelleth towards the land of heaven;
Over the silver mountains,
Where spring the nectar fountains:
    There will I kiss
    The bowl of bliss;
And drink mine everlasting fill
Upon every milken hill.
My soul will be a-dry before;
But after, it will thirst no more."

SIR WALTER RALEIGH

...I was sore delayed on the road, owing to the mires about Winchester, and it was the morning of Thursday, October the 28th, before I arrived in London. I went straight to my lady Raleigh's lodgings in Broad Street, that I might comfort my dear cousin. On the way I had heard the issue of the trial, and how Sir Walter was to be executed the next morning. 'Twas no surprise, for His Majesty had resolved at all costs on friendship with Spain, and the voice of Count Gondomar had more authority than any Englishman's. But so slender was the case that the Court dare not condemn him for his Guiana voyage, seeing that if he had shed Spanish blood 'twas because his journey was opposed, and all England held that Spain had no better title to Guiana than to Kent. So they fell back upon the old trial, fifteen years before, and he was judged to die by reason of his share in Cobham's plot. I leave future ages to approve the honesty of such a course. Sir Walter was to perish that Spain might be appeased, but the charge on which he fell was that once he had been too good a friend to Spain! I envy not the conscience of those who compassed this pitiful folly.

I found my cousin Bess sore shrunken with grief, but sustained by that great heart which for twenty years of stress had never failed her. She had lived so long in suspense that the worst was no new thing, and she bore it as one who has ever been an intimate of sorrow. My lady Astley was with her, the wife of the lieutenant of the Tower, who had been a good friend to Sir Walter in those last days. 'Twas her daughter Lucy that became the wife of that noted soldier, Colonel Hutchinson, who in after years held Nottingham Castle against King Charles.

In the evening Sir Walter was brought to the Gate-house of St Peter at Westminster, and Bess and I set out to visit him. 'Twas a rainy night, and round the gateway stood a press of citizens, eager to have news of the prisoner, for he was dearly loved by the common folk. Heads were bared as Bess entered, and there were cries of wrath and regret. "Bid Sir Walter be of good cheer," one fellow whispered; "for he leaves a name that will never be wiped out of English hearts."

To my amazement, we found him seated amid a group of friends, cheerfully taking tobacco. His countenance these latter years had been often heavy and his eye wild and restless. But now 'twas as if some kind hand had smoothed the lines from his brow. He seemed younger than he had looked since I saw him enter London after his Cadiz fight. His eye was mild and peaceful, but grave, as became one on the threshold of eternity. Yet as he set a chair for his wife there was merriment in it.

"There is scant room for the spectators at tomorrow's play," he said. "I have been warning Sir Hugh to come in good time if he would make sure of a place. I alone need have no fears on that score."

But when he saw my clouded brow he patted me on the shoulder and bade me be cheerful.

"Grieve not for me, Francis," he said. "What is this world but a larger prison, out of which some are daily chosen for execution? I am the fortunate one to die with my good friends around me. It might have been in a Guiana swamp or in some gale of the Ocean, where I would have had scant time to think of heaven."

Francis Thyn, my cousin, who did not cease to weep with his head in his hands, counselled him not to carry himself with too much bravery. "Your enemies have ever accused you of pride," he said, "and it is seemly to go to God with a grave spirit."

Sir Walter laughed. "Fear not, dear cousin. I am merry because I have little to sorrow for. Of late I am the less fit for labour, and I welcome Death, which gives me rest. 'Tis my last mirth; do not grudge it me. I grieve to part from you, my true wife and my true comrades, but it must not be said that Raleigh feared what he so often dared. I would have England see me go joyfully to my end, that she may honour the faith that can support a man both in life and death. 'Tis my testament, dear lad, the little all I have to leave."

Wine was brought, and he pledged us in a cup. "To the Indies," he drank, "which the English shall yet possess! To the brave fellows who will yet sail to the West with better fortunes than me!"

Then he asked that all should leave him, save Bess and me and Doctor Tounson, the Dean of Westminster, whom the Council had appointed to attend him. The Dean inquired into his spiritual state. He answered with reverence, saying that he was persuaded that no man that loved God and feared Him could die with cheerfulness and courage, except he were assured of God's love and favour. I have never seen a resolution so calm and heavenly. The Dean would have encouraged him against the fear of death, but Sir Walter answered that he had no fear. "The manner of my death," he said, "may seem grievous to others, but for myself I would rather die so than of a burning fever. My soul will be my own till the steel falls." Then he gave to the Dean his Bible to keep as a remembrance. In it he had written some lines which I transcribe:

> "Even such is time, that takes in trust
>   Our youth, or joys, our all we have,
>   And pays us but with age and dust;
>   Who in the dark and silent grave,
>   When we have wandered all our ways,
>   Shuts up the story of our days!
>   But from this earth, this grave, this dust,
>   The Lord shall raise me up, I trust."

After this Doctor Tounson left, and he was alone with Bess and me. He embraced his wife, stroking her hair, and saying that to leave her was the only bitterness of death. I mind that she wept sore, a thing I had not marked before in her, for she was a woman of great strength of soul. "For thirty years, dear heart," he said, "you have been my true comrade, and have ever sweetened my sorrows and doubled my joys. I have so ordered things that you may live out the days yet left to you in a little ease, and Francis will guide your small estate well. I leave you the charge of our son, and the care of my memory. Be not lonely, dear wife, for God's good angels will be near you, and in a little time we will be joined in Paradise."

I was too moved to take note of what followed, but I mind that she asked him if he had any other words for her. He said that on the morrow he would speak from the scaffold to all England, touching the cause for which he died, but to her he needed no defence. Then he remembered something about an Irish debt which he bade me discharge, and he besought me to do something for the memory of Captain Keymis. His one regret was that he had used harsh speech to him on the Guiana voyage, and he would fain have undone it.

The hour of twelve struck from St Peter's clock, and Bess declared that he must rest. Her tears broke out afresh at the parting, and she told him that she had leave to bury his body. "It is well, dear Bess," he said, smiling, "that thou mayst dispose of that dead which thou hadst not always the disposing of when alive." And when she had almost swooned, he held her in his arms and bade her show her courage to the last. " 'Tis no true parting, sweet lass," he said, "for the living and the dead are alike in God's keeping."

But I think his philosophy was near breaking. For as I led her out of the chamber, he looked after her with anguished eyes, as knowing that he would never see her again on earth.

I left Bess with my lady Astley praying by her side, and reached the Gate-house by seven o'clock of a raw autumn morn. I had a warrant from the Council for admission, and found Sir Walter busy with his dressing. He had donned his richest suit, for, as he said, he would not dress less nobly for death than for a bridal. He wore, I remember, a yellow satin doublet and breeches of black taffeta and silk stockings, and over all a black wrought velvet night-gown. Likewise on account of his ague he had a laced skull-cap. He ate a hearty breakfast, and smoked a pipe of tobacco, as if he were at Sherborne with a summer's day before him and no more care than the ordering of his gardens.

About the hour of nine the Sheriffs and their men arrived, and bade him make ready to attend them. The jailer of the Gate-house, who loved him deeply, brought a cup of hot sack against the chill of the morning. He drank it gladly, and when asked if it were to his liking, he said: "I will answer you as did the fellow who drank of St Giles' bowl as he went to Tyburn: ' 'Tis good drink,' he said, 'if a man might but tarry by it.' " Then he bade me farewell, kissing me on both cheeks; and with a great beating of drums he was gone.

I had a seat provided in Sir Randolph Carew's balcony, but I chose rather to join the press around the scaffold, that I might be near to Sir Walter at the end. There was a mightly crowd of folk, among whom I saw old sailormen and grim bronzed fellows from the ports, whose mouths were set sternly as if to choke back tears. Far off from Citywards came the jangling of bells, for 'twas the day of the Lord Mayor's procession; but that must have been an empty show, for near all London was assembled in Palace Yard, and the barriers which had been built were swept away like sandhills by the tide. The scaffold was close in front of the Parliament House, where Sir Walter had once his seat. A fire burned by it for the Sheriffs to warm themselves at, and as he mounted the steps, Sir Walter held his hands to the blaze. The ague was ever on him, and I knew that he feared lest a fit should take him and choke his utterance.

My lords Northampton and Doncaster and Arundel, who had found monies for the Guiana voyage, ascended the scaffold and shook Raleigh's hand. I remember that in the crowd that pressed about his foot there was an old man with a bald head. Sir Walter noted him, and asked why he ventured out on such a morning. "For no reason," said the old man, "but to see you and pray God for you." Whereupon Sir Walter took his laced cap from his head and flung it to him. "Take it, my friend," he cried, "for you need it now more than I." The fellow received it gladly, but did not don it. He folded it reverently and placed it in his bosom.

Then Raleigh began to speak. At first his voice was hoarse with the cold, and his face wan and pinched like one with the ague. But as he continued his voice cleared, his colour returned, and once again he had the air of youth and freedom that I remembered on the night before. He began by thanking God that He had sent him to die in the light before an assembly of honourable witnesses, and that his fever had not taken him at the time. Then he told the story of the Guiana voyage, and rebutted the charge of such as thought him in intriguer with France or a reviler of the King. "It is no time for me to flatter or to fear princes," he said, "I who am subject only unto Death; yet, if I ever spake disloyally or dishonestly of the King, the Lord blot me out of His Book of Life!"

He spoke of his purposes in the Guiana voyage, and called on my lord Arundel to bear witness that he had ever promised to return, whether he failed or succeeded. He told how the crew of the *Destiny* would fain have kept him out of England, unless he had striven with them and won their consent to go back. Then he spoke of my lord Essex's death, and his voice faltered. There were some that said he had slighted the Earl at his execution. "Nay," he cried, "rather I bewailed him with tears. Though I was of a contrary faction, yet I knew well that his enemies were my enemies, and 'twas those who did him to death who later pulled me down."

Last, in a hush so deep that the striking of the hour from St Peter's Church was like the trump of doom, he sought from all pardon and prayers. He said: "I entreat that you will all join with me in prayer to the great God of Heaven, whom I have grievously offended, for I have been a soldier, a sailor, and a courtier, which are courses of wickedness and vice… I have a long journey to take, and must bid the company farewell. I have been a man of many ventures, and now I embark on the last and longest. So I take my leave of you, making my peace with God."

The Sheriffs bade all depart from the scaffold, and there were left only Sir Walter, the Dean, and the headsman. The press of the throng had brought me close under the bars, and I could mark every line of Raleigh's face. While all men were sobered and solemnized by his words, many weeping silently, he himself bore a bright and cheerful countenance. I was so taken by the sight that I forgot sorrow. Nay, there seemed no cause to sorrow, for the man was all radiant and joyful, like a youth setting out on a happy enterprise.

He gave his hat and some money to the attendants who had been with him at the Gatehouse, and then prepared himself without assistance for the block. He took off his gown and doublet and bared his neck. I noticed how brown was the upper part where the wind and sun had beaten, and how white the lower. 'Twas like a line to guide the hand of Death.

He called for the axe, and the headsman, a lean bowed fellow much overcome by the occasion, fumbled and would have denied it. Raleigh chid him, "Do you think I am a babe to fear steel?" he asked.

He ran his finger down the edge, and turned to the Sheriffs with a smile. " 'Tis a sharp medicine, but 'tis a sure cure of all diseases."

After he went to the four corners of the scaffold and spoke to the crowd. He asked their pardon for what he had done amiss in life, and besought them to remember the good and forget the ill. "Cherish my dreams," he said. "I am like the man in the fairy tale who dreamed true, though he had nothing but blows for it." He asked them to pray to God to bestow on him strength. To my lord Arundel he said something which I could not catch, but which I judged was a message to the King. Last, the Dean asked him in what faith he died. He replied that he was of the faith of the Church of England, and hoped to have all his sins washed away by the precious blood of our Saviour Christ.

Then I think my eyes dazzled, and I seemed to see him larger than mortal above that multitude. Save that figure on the scaffold all the world went small. The Dean was but a bent old man, with silly eyes. The headsman and the Sheriffs were things of straw and tinsel. The Lords in the balconies were hollow creatures, all fearful and craven. The great throng was made up of weary broken folk, sheep with no shepherd. 'Twas an assemblage of death-heads; only Raleigh lived; only he was young and strong and joyful. I was in a trance like St Paul, and seemed to see for one moment how Sir Walter's future fame would rise to comfort this realm of England. I was pressed close under the bars of the scaffold, and by stretching my hand could almost have touched his feet. I looked up into his face, and, like Stephen's, it was transfigured. Aforetime there had been a petulance in the lips and a pride in the eye: but all was cleared, so that it shone with good-will and the peace of God.

In a dream I heard words. The headsman spread a cloak for him to kneel on, and besought his pardon. Raleigh put his hand on the man's shoulder and forgave him. Then the Dean would have him lay his head on the block with the face to the East. Sir Walter, smiling, asked, "What matter how the head lies so the heart be right?" but did the Dean's will. He was offered a bandage for the eyes, which he put away. "Think you," he asked, "that I fear the shadow of the axe when I fear not the substance?"

He kneeled and laid his head on the block, and as he kneeled he cried to the people, "Give me heartily your prayers." There was no answer, but a sobbing like the wind in trees.

He bade the headsman strike when he should hold forth his hands. His lips moved as if in prayer. I had no fear or sorrow, for what I saw seemed to me too glorious for sadness.

The signal was given, but the headsman, who shook like an aspen, did not stir.

"Strike, man, strike!" cried Sir Walter. "What dost thou fear?" They were his last words.

The blow fell, and then a second, and the head was severed from the body. As it dropped the lips moved, still in prayer.

Then my trance departed, and mortal sorrow flowed over my heart. As I turned, my eyes blind with tears, I heard the headsman's voice, hoarse and weak as if it feared the lie – "This is the head of a traitor!"

1 Francis Champernoun wrote this chapter and the one following, and left them as a bequest to his children. A hundred years afterwards the Reverend Launcelot Matthews incorporated, by permission of the family, certain passages from the narrative in his *Itinerarium Devoniae*.

CHAPTER 11

"A Better Indies than the King of Spain's"
(1619)

"The greatest honour that ever belonged to the greatest Monarkes was the inlarging their Dominions, and erecting Commonweales."

CAPTAIN JOHN SMITH

…On a mild afternoon in early April we came out of the wolds which stretch east and west from Shaftesbury, and entered the pleasant vale of Sherborne. Of old the manor belonged to Sir Walter Raleigh, but now my lord Digby had it from the King. There rode with me my cousin Bess, whom I carried to my house at Greenway in Devon that she might find there a quiet retreat after the troublous years she had known. As we topped the hill, and saw the meads and plantations and the shining stream all yellow in the April sunlight, we reined up in a sudden sorrow. I have always held Sherborne the true march of the West Country, where something of our mellow Devon air begins to temper the bleak downs of Dorset. For certain I have never seen the vale more fair than on this afternoon. The Castle lay silent, for my lord was ever about the Court, and was but now back in England from Spain. But I marked the gardens Sir Walter had planted, and especially the terrace, where I have often walked with him and listened to his discourse. Every stone of the house was of his building, and every lawn called him its creator. For myself, I choked at the sight, and Bess wept as if her heart would break.

I bade her dismount, and gave the horses to a groom's charge, while I led her to a little hillock beside the highway. I was never one to chide sorrow, for I hold that to grieve is a natural comfort. All that day Bess had been in better heart, full of plans for her boy Carew, and ready to welcome the peace of Greenway. But now, at the sight of Sherborne, she was back among the pitiful events of the autumn, when the noblest head in England fell. She turned weeping eyes to the gardens, where once she had drunk her fill of happiness, and, sobbing bitterly, she told of this and that; how Sir Walter had planned a new fish-pond, and planted a long alley of cypress. Then she fell silent, for steps were coming down the road.

'Twas an old, grizzled fellow, who walked lame, as if from a long journey. He stumped along very cheerfully, whistling an air beloved by Devon sailors, *The Almiranty of Santa Fee*. He had writ large on him the marks of the sea, in his mahogany cheek, his clear blue eye, and the bleached hair which comes from Tropic suns. Such figures as his have grown scarce in these days, and the sight of him lightened my heaviness. He came abreast of us, pulled off his hat, and would have passed on, when he looked at Bess and stopped short of a sudden.

Bess turned her sorrowful eyes on him; but he never looked at her face. His gaze was fixed on her bosom, where hung a little jewel of gold, which Sir Walter had prized greatly, and wore always next to his heart. He stammered and took a step forward; then halted and stared blankly.

"The jewel!" he muttered, "Sir Walter's jewel! You have the charm lady."

Bess rose and held our her hand.

"I wear Sir Walter's jewel, good friend, because I was once Sir Walter's wife."

At this the seaman was on his knees in the dust, kissing her hand.

"O my lady, my lady!" he cried; "I have never clapped eyes on you before, but I was an old seaman of Raleigh's, and he showed me that charm in Guiana. 'Tis the charm for El Dorado my lady."

"He has gone thither," she said, "and hath no longer need of a charm."

I think the sight of the old sailor had braced her to a better mood.

"True, true, mistress," he said; "that is a brave soul. I am old Nathan Stubbs, who adventured with him to Guiana twenty years ago, and fought with him at Cadiz and in the Islands. I have sailed many voyages, but for me he was my sole Captain. I am on my way back from London town, where I journeyed to see the last of him."

"But that was six months since," I said.

"True, sir," he nodded; "but travelling for a poor man is slow work, and I have a foolish leg. The worst of the way is by now, and I shall be home by the week's end."

This he said in a tone of merriment, but I could see by the leanness of his body that the journey had been as hard as it had been slow.

"There be loyal men left in the West," I said.

"There were a thousand who would have walked for Sir Walter to the world's end," he answered. "But some had wives, and some had young children, and some were too poor to buy provender, and only Nathan Stubbs, who calls no man or woman master, had luck to go. What a fortunate man I be!"

"And now?" I asked.

"Why, now I go back to Budleigh, to bide the rest of my days in the house which my uncle Noah bequeathed me. I am too old for voyages, and there be no captains to sail with. I will smoke my pipe on the harbour wall, and tell my tales to the young, in the hope that I may breed up another John Hawkins or Francis Drake.

For another Raleigh I have no hope, for his like comes not again."

He sat himself down on the grass beside us and pulled forth a great brass tobacco-box. When he had lit his pipe, he inquired of me the name of the castle in the trees.

I told him it was Sherborne, a former house of Sir Walter's.

"Ay," said he, "I have heard on't. Sir Walter had many dwellings in his day, but he had but the one home. The King could take his manors, but could not make him homeless."

Bess looked up at him, and asked of what he spoke.

"Why, my lady, as I read it, Sir Walter had but one home, and that was the sea. Or, maybe 'twas in the Western lands where his fancy ever turned. But 'twas not in England, or in any stone walls or green gardens, though he loved them well."

Bess smiled through half-shed tears.

"That is a comforting thought, Master Stubbs. I have been looking at Sherborne, and grieving for the happy days that are past, and the fair estate that is now another's. But you say truly. Sir Walter had a better estate, which none could take from him."

"Ay, and 'tis still his, and his spirit holds it in trust for England. Look you, my lady, when I saw Sir Walter's head fall I was out of my mind with sorrow. With some old comrades we sought our lodging in Wapping, and would have plotted a great slaughter of them who had compassed the crime. But by good fortune I slept on the matter, and in the morning I was come to a better mind. For thus I reasoned with myself. Those who have taken his life have done him the best service. There is no honest soul in England but thrills with the shame of it, and glories in so proud a death. A spirit is abroad which will breed and multiply, and will yet do more than Raleigh did in that cause he loved. So I says to myself, 'Nathan Stubbs,' I says, 'it ill becomes an ignorant man such as you to be interfering with the wise ways of the Almightly.' So I held back the others from violence, and beyond a broken head or two London took no hurt of us. We are scattered now, and I am hobbling back to Budleigh; but all the way I have cheered my heart with the promise. I have been in Virginia, my lady, and seen the noble rivers, and the forests of tall trees, and the plains of deep grass. Some day we English will dwell there, and build a new nation. Ay, and wherever on the earth there is a fine land to be made out of the wilderness our children will plant the English flag."

He swung to his feet and looked into the West, where the sun was now beginning to decline.

"There is a short path to Axminster near by, and I must be well on the road to Misteron before the darkening. Fare-you-well, my lady. It is like we will never meet on earth, but Nathan Stubbs gives you his word of comfort for a sore heart. 'Tis Sir Walter's saying: keep in mind those better Indies than the King of Spain's."

As we watched the steadfast old figure plodding down the road Bess laid her hand on my arm and smiled.

"God has sent me a true consoler," she said. "I weep no more for Sherborne. Nay, I rejoice that Sir Walter hath left to us and to all England an inheritance so princely."

John Buchan

Julius Caesar

John Buchan wrote of Caesar 'He performed the greatest constructive task ever achieved by human hands. He drew the habitable earth into an empire which lasted for five centuries, and he laid the foundations of a fabric of law and government which is still standing after two thousand years.'

In this romantic biography Buchan attempts to understand the hidden thoughts of the great soldier. He charts the tale of Caesar's youth, early political career, success, conquest of Gaul and of the world, ending with his murder at the hands of Brutus and the Republican-minded conspirators.

Gordon at Khartoum

The year is 1883 and Gladstone finds that the cutting of the Suez Canal has involved Britain irrevocably in Egypt's affairs. General Gordon, Governor of the Sudan, is sent on a mission to evacuate Khartoum. He is besieged there for ten months by the Mahdi's troops and is killed two days before a relief force arrives. This gripping historical account focuses on the bravery of this great man.

John Buchan

Oliver Cromwell

John Buchan sets out to redress popular opinion of this English soldier and statesman. His biography achieves that aim, starting with Cromwell's childhood and youth.

Born in 1599, Cromwell was a devout Puritan who, when war broke out, formed his Ironsides. He won the battles of Marston Moor and Naseby and brought Charles I to trial. After establishing the Commonwealth, he suppressed the Levellers, Ireland and the Scots. In 1653, five years before his death, he established a Protectorate.

John Buchan wrote of Cromwell 'He is a soldier now on the grand scale, strategist as well as tactician, statesman as well as fighting man, and it is by this new phase of his military career that his place is to be adjudged in the hierarchy of the great captains'.

The King's Grace

This sympathetic portrait starts with the death of Edward VII and George V's succession. It was a reign that saw many changes including the Union of South Africa, the First World War and the General Strike of 1926.

John Buchan wrote that 'This book is not a biography of King George, but an attempt to provide a picture – and some slight interpretation – of his reign, with the Throne as the continuing thing through an epoch of unprecedented change.'

John Buchan

Montrose

This is a compassionate biography of the legendary Scottish commander, James Graham, Marquis of Montrose. John Buchan describes Montrose's command of the royalist forces during the 1644 to 1650 war with the Covenanters. Montrose's exceptional strength, leadership and military genius are brought to life. Buchan also illustrates an important period in Scottish history, adding his own measure of adventure to this study.

The Clearing House

This anthology of extracts from Buchan's writings is well worth reading for its historical range and wide selection of subjects close to the author's heart. Alongside portraits of Julius Caesar, Cleopatra, Virgil, Cromwell and Sir Walter Scott, to name but five, are lyrical descriptions of landscapes. Buchan's love for the great outdoors comes to the fore in his account of the African veld and in the more domestic *Wood, Sea and Hill*. There are also short essays on fishing, shooting and golf, among other sports.

914806

Printed in Great Britain by
Amazon.co.uk, Ltd.,
Marston Gate.